Woman TO Woman

Woman TO Woman

A Guide to Teaching and Leading Women

Edited by Debbie Bumbalough and Dwina Willis

Gospel Advocate Company
Nashville, Tennessee

Published by Gospel Advocate Co.
1006 Elm Hill Pike, Nashville, TN 37210
http://www.gospeladvocate.com

ISBN-10: 0-89225-557-9
ISBN-13: 978-0-89225-557-3

Dedication

This book is dedicated to all of the women and teachers who have been a strong influence in our lives. They have taught us how to study the Word, apply it in our daily lives, and then by example how to live for Him.

We want to thank our families for their unchanging support. David and Mike are truly two spiritual companions that lift us up. We also want to thank Kerry G. Anderson, president of Gospel Advocate, for his encouragement to take our study for women and make it into a book.

A sincere thank you to all of the wonderful women who contributed to *Woman to Woman*. Each has her own unique talents and abilities that she has lent to the Lord.

A special thank you to managing editor Debra G. Wright and the editorial staff at the Gospel Advocate and everyone else who helped edit *Woman to Woman*.

Our sincere desire is for women to realize that they are valued members of the Lord's church. We pray that all of us will continue to identify and use our God-given talents in His service.

Debbie Bumbalough
Dwina Willis

Table of Contents

Introduction

Chapter 1

Using Your Talents

Dwina Willis

H ow have women throughout history used their talents to glorify God? What is the niche in the kingdom where their talents will best be used? These are questions women ask again and again as we strive to serve God to the best of our abilities. The answer to the last question will vary from woman to woman because our talents differ. The question should not be, "Will I serve God?" Instead it should be, "How and where will I serve God?"

Biblical Examples

Jesus is our example in all things. Using our time and talents is no exception. In John 9:4, He said, "I must work the works of Him who sent Me, while it is day." We, too, must take advantage of opportunities as they occur. Jesus "went about doing good" (Acts 10:38). We, too, should seek opportunities to do good. Christian women today should heed the advice Jesus gave in Luke 10:25-37 to a lawyer who asked what he must do to inherit eternal life. Jesus answered by telling the parable of the good Samaritan. At the end of the parable, Jesus advised the lawyer, "Go and do likewise" (v. 37).

Look at some of the ways women in the Bible used their talents in serving God. In the Old Testament, women are often not the featured character in a biblical account, but there are many from whom we can learn. Rebekah was compassionate and hospitable (Genesis 24:15-28). Jochebed was courageous enough to defy the edict of Pharaoh (Exodus 2:1-10; 6:20). Miriam led the women in song after they had passed through the Red Sea (Exodus 15:20-21). Deborah was a poet and a judge. She gained the admiration and affection of her people and was called a "mother in Israel" (Judges 5:7). Abigail had the gift of wisdom and discernment (1 Samuel 25:2-42). Ruth was virtuous, kind to Naomi, and had a work ethic, all of which caused her to be noticed by Boaz (Ruth 3:11).

In the New Testament, Mary, the mother of Jesus, had a submissive spirit that allowed her to say to God, "Behold the maidservant of the Lord! Let it be to me according to your word" (Luke 1:38). How many of us have that attitude when it comes to God's will and God's work?

Women were actively serving the Lord before the church was established. Mary and Martha offered Jesus hospitality and in turn were taught by Him (Luke 10:38-42). Women anointed Him (Luke 7:36-38; John 12:2-8). Mary Magdalene, Joanna, Susanna and others provided for Jesus financially (Luke 8:2-3). Finally, women were present at the crucifixion and were the first to see the risen Lord (John 19:25; 20:11-18).

Consider the examples women set in the early church. Priscilla and her husband, Aquila, took Apollos aside and taught him about the baptism of Jesus (Acts 18:24-26). They were called "fellow workers" by Paul because they risked their own necks for his life (Romans 16:3-4).

Hospitality must have been customary in the home of Mary, the mother of John Mark. When Peter was released from prison, he went to her house and found people had gathered there to pray (Acts 12:12). After her conversion on the riverbank in Philippi, Lydia opened her home to Paul and his companions (Acts 16:11-15). Dorcas was loved because of the garments she made for the widows of Joppa (Acts 9:36-43). Phoebe is described as a sister, a servant and a "helper of many" (Romans 16:1-2). Lois and Eunice grounded Timothy in the faith (2 Timothy 1:5).

Several other women are briefly mentioned in Romans 16. Paul does not tell us specifically what they did, but the fact that their work is commended suggests they had been faithful and unwavering in their service to the Lord.

These women did not all do the same things. Their talents lay in different venues. They served God in a variety of ways, but they all did something. Moses made excuses to get out of serving God (Exodus 3-4), but these women did what they could (Mark 14:8).

There has always been a place for women in the Lord's kingdom. Jesus saw women as valued members of His church, but He also gave guidelines under which women are to work, worship and learn in the church (1 Corinthians 11:3-16; 14:26-35; 1 Timothy 2:9-15). Women are commanded to teach (Titus 2:3-5), but we must work within the boundaries God has set. We need to focus on identifying and using our talents for God's glory (Matthew 5:16).[1]

Analogy of the Body

In 1 Corinthians 12, Paul compares the church to the human body. In the human body, there are many different types of tissues, organs and organ systems. Each organ or organ system has a specific job to do. If all the organs are working correctly and performing the appropriate tasks, the body stays healthy. If only one organ is not working correctly, the whole body can suffer.

I teach a human biology class. In our textbook[2] at the end of each chapter covering an organ system, the author has a page that puts the system into perspective. It tells how one system impacts the other systems and what all other systems do that affect that particular system. No system in the human body stands alone. Some systems, like the cardiovascular system, may be better known than others, such as the urinary or lymphatic systems. However, if the kidneys fail to filter the blood, their importance becomes apparent. Each system is essential if the body is to work as God designed.

The same is true in the church. "There are diversities of gifts, but the same Spirit. There are differences of ministries, but the same Lord. And there are diversities of activities, but it is the same God who works all in all" (1 Corinthians 12:4-6). It is important that each member do what she was designed to do. Just because someone is not working in your favorite area of ministry doesn't mean she is not serving God. We do not all accomplish the same things, and that's fine. God designed us to be different. If even one person is not functioning as God planned, however, the whole church suffers. Each member is essential if Christ's body is to work effectively.

> For as the body is one and has many members, but all the members of that one body, being many, are one body, so also is Christ. … For in fact the body is not one member but many. If the foot should say, "Because I am not a hand, I am not of the body," is it therefore not of the body? And if the ear should say, "Because I am not an eye, I am not of the body," is it therefore not of the body? If the whole body were an eye, where would be the hearing? If the whole were hearing, where would be the smelling? But now God has set the members, each one of them, in the body just as He pleased. And if they were all one member, where would the body be? But now indeed there are many members, yet one body. … Now you are the body of Christ, and members individually. (1 Corinthians 12:12, 14-20, 27)

The Parable of the Talents

In Matthew 25:14-30, we read the parable of the talents. One servant was given five talents, another was given two, and another was given one talent "each according to his own ability" (v. 15). The servants with five and two talents used their talents and gained more. The servant with one was fearful and buried his talent. The first two were commended and rewarded for their work. The one-talent man was cast into outer darkness because he was too lazy to use his talent (v. 26). His talent was given to the five-talent man.

Is it possible if we use our talents, we may gain more? We may find the courage to step out of our comfort zone and try new things. We may find undiscovered talents that may be harnessed for God's service. We may learn how to do things allowing us to serve God in a new way. Will you be like the five-talent and two-talent men, or are you too fearful and lazy to use the gifts given to you by God?

What Now?

In the following chapters of this book, you will be challenged to get outside your comfort zone. Lead a prayer, lead a song, or teach a lesson in your ladies Bible class or at the next ladies day. Do not use excuses like Moses. Do not be like that one-talent man. At least try. Remember what Paul wrote, "Be anxious for nothing, but in everything by prayer and supplication, with thanksgiving, let your requests be made known to God; and the peace of God, which surpasses all understanding, will guard your hearts and minds through Christ Jesus. … I can do all things through Christ who strengthens me" (Philippians 4:6-7, 13). With a confident faith in our God, we can do more than we ever imagined.

Not all women are cut out to be song leaders or class teachers, but how will you know unless you try? If your talents lie elsewhere, use those talents to the best of your ability. Pamela Stewart, in *Evangelistic Women*,[3] studies several areas of service for women. She mentions family ministry, hospitality, teaching, benevolence, counseling, encouragement, working with the aging, missions, writing for publications, and more. There is so much work for women to do in God's kingdom. Find your niche and work. You will find joy in service.

God loved us enough to send His best, His one and only Son (1 John 4:9). Should not that motivate us to give our best to God? Let the love you have for God, His kingdom and His children motivate you to reflect God to the world around you (Matthew 22:36-39; John 13:35; 1 Corinthians 13; 1 John 4:7-21). Use your talents so the world "may see your good works and glorify your Father in heaven" (Matthew 5:16).

Activities

1. What are some of the talents women of the Bible exhibited? Do you have some of these same talents?

2. What are some of the guidelines under which women are to work, worship and learn in the church?

3. Using the analogy of the body, why is it important that every member of Christ's body use the talents given to him/her?

4. What talents have you been given? Have you been hiding your talents or using them? How can you use your talents to serve God?

5. Should we try new avenues of service? Why or why not?

6. Discuss the ministries given by Pamela Stewart in her book *Evangelistic Women*. Can you find a niche where you can serve in that list?

Chapter 2

Ladies Bible Class – A Three-Legged Stool

Rosemary McKnight

H ave you ever been a part of a Bible class that you looked forward to each week? Did you feel that meeting to study the Bible with other Christian women was one of the highlights of your week? I was fortunate to be a part of such a class. At the time I was a young married woman expecting our first child. My husband and I were six hours away from the nearest relative, so the women in the Wednesday night ladies class became my family.

Sue Crabtree taught the class. Twenty-five years later I still have the notes from her study of the Old Testament. I vividly remember the enthusiasm she brought to class each week. She made every woman feel special and like an important part of the class. Most of all, Sue challenged us spiritually. She made me want to study the Bible on my own, and she made the lessons relevant to my life.

What can we do to have ladies classes like that today? How do we meet the diverse needs of women attending the class?

A ladies class should be like a three-legged stool to be successful. If one leg of a three-legged stool breaks, the stool collapses. For the stool to work properly, all three legs need to be firmly in place. Three different legs need to be in place if a ladies class is going to be dynamic – Bible study, fellowship and outreach.

Bible Study

The purpose of a Bible class is to learn more about God's Word. Teachers must take their responsibility seriously. James 3:1 says, "My brethren, let not many of you become teachers, knowing that we shall receive a stricter judgment."

Ladies classes have sometimes been criticized for having too much fluff and not enough substance. Teachers need to make sure the study is biblical. The studies may vary from textual to topical, but all class studies need to be based on God's Word. Titus 2 describes qualities of a sound church. Paul writes in Titus 2:1, "But as for you, speak the things which are proper for sound doctrine." All Bible classes need to be teaching sound biblical principles. Many Bible classes today need less "I think …" and more of "The Bible says …" in their discussions.

One of the most difficult decisions to make is deciding what to study. Most classes are composed of women of different ages, backgrounds and spiritual needs. It is hard to choose a study that meets the needs of every member of the class. Doing a written survey occasionally is helpful. Ask women what they want or need to study. It may be wise to alternate a textual study and a topical study. Some studies may work best if the same teacher teaches the entire study, while others may work well using different women in the class as teachers.

Teachers who use a study book in class should read the book before they teach it. Look for doctrinal errors. Many good books are available for study, but be cautious. Make sure your study book has sound doctrine.

The study should also be practical. Several years ago I conducted a survey to find out what makes a dynamic ladies class. The number one answer was studying topics that relate to everyday life. Women want to know that the Bible can make a difference in their lives. Each lesson needs some practical applications. Even textual studies should show how the Bible is relevant today. What good is knowledge if we do not know how to apply it?

Bible classes need participation from the members of the class. When I asked women what made a dynamic class, the second and third most commonly mentioned items were well-prepared, enthusiastic teachers and lots of participation from the class. Teachers, remember that this is not your class. It is their (the members') class. Class discussions allow ladies to study scriptures from different perspectives and share how they have applied God's Word in their lives. Members of the class are more likely to study and prepare for the lesson if they know they will be asked to participate.

One of the goals of Bible class is to challenge members to study on their own. Teachers should want their class members to be like the Bereans mentioned in Acts 17. They eagerly received the words that were taught, but they also examined the Scriptures themselves to see if the truth was being taught (v. 11). Memory verses are used in children's classes, but why not adult classes? Quoting scripture together is one way to involve all the members of the class and get them to study on their own.

Classes that are biblical, practical and involve the members of the class have one leg of the three-legged stool.

Fellowship

The second leg of the stool is fellowship among members of the class. Ladies need and want to feel that they are accepted and that people in the Bible class care about them. One purpose of class is Bible study, but another purpose is to encourage one another.

> And let us consider one another in order to stir up love and good works, not forsaking the assembling of ourselves together, as is the manner of some, but exhorting one another, and so much the more as you see the Day approaching. (Hebrews 10:24-25)

The fellowship of a ladies class is a wonderful way to build bonds between older and younger women. I love ladies classes that include women of all ages. The wisdom and experience of older ladies and the exuberance of younger women can blend together to create lifelong friendships. A class on parenting may not be applicable to older women, but think of the lessons they can share from their experience of raising their children! A ladies class is a safe haven for women whose husbands are not Christians and won't come to church with them, as well as for single women and widows. A healthy dynamic is added to a class when different ages, backgrounds and perspectives are brought to Bible study.

Fellowship takes place during the class period and should extend to times outside of class. The teacher needs to be early and greet class members as they arrive. Visitors should be met and introduced to the class. Recognize birthdays, anniversaries, new parents, grandparents, honors or other reasons class members have to celebrate. A ladies class is also a place where women can share concerns and sorrows. Singing together is a great way to begin each class. Take a few minutes to discuss class news. Meet the needs of members whether it be through cards, money, food, bridal or baby showers, etc. Create an atmosphere of warmth, acceptance and joy.

One of the greatest areas of fellowship takes place when ladies pray together. Some of the most meaningful time in class will be time spent in prayer as women pour their hearts out to God. A bond is created when women pray together and see those prayers answered. Take time to acknowledge those answered prayers in class and give God the glory. Always ask someone to lead prayer before class begins. Don't embarrass someone who may feel uncomfortable leading prayer by calling on her in front of the class.

Fellowship may extend beyond class time through activities such as secret pal programs; ladies night out; Bible times parties; mother-daughter events; hosting a tea for teens, widows or graduates; making crafts; planning a ladies day; or having a work night. Activities outside the classroom are especially important for women who can't attend the weekly ladies class because they are teaching children during that time period or who have to work during the allotted time. These activities allow women to see each other in a different way. They can laugh together and have opportunities to get to know each other better. Women who study the Bible together, pray together, and have fun together will grow closer to God and one another. They will be there for each other when a need arises.

Outreach

The third leg of the stool is outreach. Ladies must take what they learn in class and apply it. It should not stay within the walls of the classroom.

> And let us not grow weary while doing good, for in due season we shall reap if we do not lose heart. Therefore, as we have opportunity, let us do good to all, especially to those who are of the household of faith. (Galatians 6:9-10)

The outreach of a ladies class may extend to others in the congregation or to those outside the church. When a need is made known, ladies classes should be quick to respond.

Missionaries appreciate the encouragement from ladies classes. A different member of the class can write a missionary each week. Care packages can be sent with items missionaries cannot purchase where they live. Remember them on their birthdays, anniversaries and other special occasions. One class made a friendship quilt for the missionary their congregation supported.

Many women cannot go on a mission trip, but they are willing to help by giving money to help a class member go or by donating items to use on a mission trip. A class can supply teaching aids, Bible story books, medical supplies, and other items to be used on mission trips. A class might sponsor a child at a Christian orphanage and send money each month to provide for that child's needs.

Ladies classes have many opportunities to reach out to the community. Classes can provide food, clothing or holiday gifts for a needy family. Grocery stores often offer specials on dishes. Class members can purchase these dishes, store them, and use them when a family in the community loses their home in a fire. They can provide school supplies or coats for needy children in the area or for a children's home. Welcome baskets with a brochure about the church and times of worship services can be taken to newcomers. There may be opportunities to work with a local jail or prison ministry.

Cards are another way to reach out to members of the church and the community. Cards can be passed around and signed during the class, but ladies need to be encouraged to send cards on their own, too. A list can be provided to the class each week with names and addresses of those who are sick, grieving, away at college, or in the military who would appreciate a card or letter from members of the class.

There is no end to the areas of service that a ladies class can do. What a wonderful way to put women's talents to use for God's glory! Outreach can provide encouragement for members of the church and opportunities to teach and evangelize those outside God's kingdom.

Conclusion

A dynamic ladies Bible class needs three components: sound Bible study, fellowship and outreach. Having these three elements will help class members grow spiritually, grow closer to one another, and reach out to others. A good ladies class can make a congregation stronger.

Activities

1. Think about ladies classes you have been a part of. What made them meaningful?

2. How should a ladies class decide what to study?

3. How does a teacher meet the needs of all women in a class that is made up of diverse ages and backgrounds? What

should you do if the class studies a topic that does not apply to you or you are not interested in?

4. What are additional ways ladies can have fellowship with each other both in and out of class?

5. Name some additional outreach projects ladies classes can do. How can they be organized?

6. What makes a good Bible teacher? Make a list of attributes.

7. Name some strategies teachers can use to encourage participation in Bible class.

8. What are some ways to fellowship with women who can't attend the class?

Chapter 3

Bible
Study

Sue Crabtree

Jennifer is a new Christian. She attends Bible class on Sunday morning at her church. The class is titled, "How to Build a Great Marriage." She also attends a ladies class on Tuesday morning where the class is studying "Characteristics of a Godly Woman." On Wednesday night in class, Jennifer has another topical study. She has no knowledge of the Bible, but she has a strong desire to study, if only she knew where to begin. How will Jennifer, a working mom, ever be able to grasp the meaning of the Word of God? Where does she begin?

Useful Tools for Bible Study

There are 66 books in the Bible, and every phrase, sentence and paragraph is important. The Bible is the Word of God, and this Bible is the only way we can find the meaning of life and learn about God. The Bible is food for our souls.

As one becomes a student of the Bible, she must have materials to aid in the study. Each student should have her personal copy of the Bible along with pens, paper or notebooks. Here is a list of materials recommended for good Bible study.

• *A Bible.* Use a standard version such as New King James or New American Standard.

• *A Bible Dictionary.* A dictionary with Bible words, names, places and events will also give scripture references for your study. For example, if you wanted to know something about King Ahab, you would look up his name in a dictionary to see who he was and also to see where you could read about him in the Bible. Some people think this is the most important tool in Bible study.

• *A Concordance.* A concordance is a book with key words to help you find where a verse is located in the Bible. For example, if you know that the Bible says, "No man can serve two masters," but don't know where it is located, you might look up "man" or "masters" and the concordance will lead you to the verse. A concordance can also be used to look up a subject. If you wanted to know what the Bible says about "adultery," you would look under "adultery" and scriptures will be listed. An unabridged, complete concordance will list all scriptures in the Bible. You may have a small concordance in the back of your Bible.

• *An Atlas.* You may have some good maps in the back of your Bible, but you still need an atlas. An atlas will give maps and information about Bible lands. An atlas also has information about Bible geography. For example, if you wanted information about the Sea of Galilee, you could look it up in an atlas and find its location along with information about the sea.

• *Other materials* such as commentaries on the books, Bible encyclopedias, different versions of the Bible, reference Bibles, or study Bibles can be very helpful. Much information is also available in Bible software sets or on the Internet.

Learning Styles

Learning styles vary by individual, and it is important to understand the differences between them to determine which is the best method for you. The three sensory learning styles are visual (learns by seeing), auditory (learns by hearing and talking about the learning), and kinesthetic (learns by doing.) Often an individual is a combination of two of the styles.

• *Visual learners* might enjoy watching movies about Bible history. The *Visual Bible* series on DVD is recommended because only the text of the Bible is used as script. Visual learners will also enjoy reading the text of the Bible.

• *Auditory learners* might enjoy listening to cassette tapes or CDs, and they need to communicate with someone about their study. Having a study partner is good for an auditory learner.

• *Kinesthetic learners* need colored pens, index cards, and activities involving their Bible study where they participate in the learning.

A Time for Bible Study

We live in busy times, and the Bible will be left on the shelf or in the car if we don't make time for Bible study. The Bible can be studied anywhere, but finding one central place with good study materials may be the best way for you to study. Some women study on their lunch hour; others study at 5:30 in the morning or at 11 at night. Set goals such as: "I will not watch television until I have completed my study" or "I will not eat breakfast until I have studied my Bible."

Each person must find the time that is best for her. If you are a morning person, probably early morning is your best time. If you stay up late, maybe before you go to bed is the best time to open God's Word.

Teaching a class of children (grades 1-6) or teaching ladies will force a good teacher to study the text of the Bible. A good teacher learns background information and the meaning of the text studied. Often studying one subject will lead one into many other studies. A well-prepared teacher is a student of the Word.

Enrolling in a Bible class at a Christian school can be motivational, challenging and helpful in looking at the text of the Bible. If you have a Christian school or college in your area, take advantage of Bible classes being offered there. Sometimes homework, challenges and written tests are given that will motivate and help the learner. There are many colleges with programs now online where one can study at home.

Good Bible Study Methods

As you begin to study the text of the Bible, you should begin with one of the Gospels. Reading an introduction to the book may be helpful. Here is a list of study methods. Pick one and try it to see if it is the right method for you.

• *Let the Bible Speak to You.* Bible study should begin with prayer. Ask God to open your mind and your heart to His Word. Read and listen to what the passage says. God's Word will unfold as you absorb the Bible through prayer, reading and study. Lay aside presuppositions. Some people study the text of the Bible forcing the scriptures to say what they want them to say or what they have always heard. We do ourselves a great disservice when we misinterpret the Scripture. As you read and study the Bible, the scriptures will begin to interpret themselves. Look at the whole passage; let it speak to you.

• *Take the Passage Apart.* This method means analyzing, synthesizing, interpreting and evaluating. It means looking at the big themes in the Bible. Journalists ask six questions, and good Bible students will ask these same six questions about the text of the Bible: Who? What? When? Where? Why? and How? The answer to every question may not be in every passage, but these questions will help you get an overview of a biblical story or biblical teaching. Bible study might be described as the process of asking questions. The more you ask, the more you may learn.

Look at the authorship, purpose, summaries and conclusions. It is very important to look at the context. Context refers to the surroundings or settings of the passage. How do the scriptures relate? What comes before the passage, and what comes after the passage? To whom was it written? What was the purpose of the writing? Remember, the scriptures do not contradict themselves. Every passage stands in relation to other passages in the Bible. Truths in the Bible are repeated over and over. If you read a scripture that seems to contradict another one in the Bible, you must look again. As you read, develop a system for marking key words and phrases in your Bible.

As you make discoveries about scriptures, you may need to consult commentaries to see what others have to say about the passages.

• *Application.* How can this scripture affect my life? How can I apply it, and how will I respond? We must draw into the scriptures personally. Moses received the Ten Commandments on the mountain. So what? How does this change my behavior? What does this story mean to me? Scriptures will not be of benefit if they are not put into my life.

• *Keeping a Journal.* As you read the Bible, write down important information. Notice events, characters, places, words and themes. Write some of these in a journal. Look up words as you study. Write down God's message for you today, principles of Christianity, promises, commands and lists. Read at least 15-30 minutes per day, and use the same amount of time to journal.

Build a Frame to Study the Text of the Bible

It is important to know what topics are covered in the Old and New Testament before one begins to study. When one builds a frame, she understands the background information of the story or book, she knows the central theme of the materials and knows the chronology of the story. When building a frame, one knows how the Bible fits together and has a knowledge of authors and purposes of writing. When a Bible frame is built, one could turn to any book in the Bible and have some idea of what the book is about and how it fits into God's plan for revelation.

New Testament Frame

One should begin Bible study in the New Testament. Here is a brief frame on which to hang a New Testament Bible study.

• *The Gospels (Matthew, Mark, Luke and John):* All four books are about the life of Christ. Matthew wrote to Jews and presented Christ as king. Mark wrote to Romans and presented Christ as a servant. Luke wrote to Greeks and presented Christ as a perfect man. John wrote to believers and presented Christ as God. John is the author who writes later, gives no parables, and is different from the other three gospels, which are known as the synoptic gospels.

• *Acts:* Written by Luke, Acts is a book of history about the early church and the activities of the apostles. It answers the question, "What must I do to be saved?" Chapters 13-18 give the missionary journeys and the activities of Paul.

• *The Epistles:* The New Testament has 21 epistles or letters written by Peter, Paul, James, John and Jude. These books are about Christian living and Christian doctrine. They give us instruction about how to live the Christian life.

Paul wrote eight letters to churches. They are known in the New Testament as Romans, 1 & 2 Corinthians, Ephesians, Philippians, Colossians, and 1 & 2 Thessalonians. Paul wrote four letters to individuals: 1 & 2 Timothy, Titus and Philemon. Paul wrote one letter to a group of churches, which is known as the book of Galatians. Hebrews is a general epistle, usually assumed to have been written by Paul.

Peter wrote 1 & 2 Peter; James wrote James; John wrote 1, 2 & 3 John; and Jude wrote Jude.

• *Revelation* is a book of prophecy and hope. Written by John, it is probably the most difficult book in the New Testament because of the symbolism contained in it.

Old Testament Frame

Much of the Old Testament is a story. A good Bible student will become familiar with the story before she begins her study of the Old Testament. Read a good Bible storybook or study survey books such as *4,000 Years in Thirteen Weeks* by Sue Crabtree to learn the story. Some know bits and pieces, but they don't know how to put the story together. Use this frame to help you.

• *Genesis:* The first book of the Old Testament covers Creation to God's people living in Egypt in peace, a time period of approximately 2,500 years. It includes stories about Adam, Noah, Abraham, Isaac, Jacob and Jacob's 12 sons.

• *Exodus:* Israelites are made slaves in Egypt where they live for 400 years. Moses leads them out of Egypt to Mt. Sinai where he received the 10 commandments and other laws.

• *Leviticus:* Not a book of history. Laws, feasts and priestly duties are covered. One major story in Chapter 10.

• *Numbers:* Moses leads the people from Mt. Sinai to the Plains of Moab. They wander in the wilderness for 40 years, and it is their children who enter the promised land.

• *Deuteronomy:* This book is a speech Moses made before he died, reviewing the past, present and future of Israel. It records the death of Moses.

• *Joshua:* Joshua takes command after Moses, conquers the land of Canaan and divides it among the tribes.

• *Judges:* The Israelites are delivered by 15 judges for 400 years in the new land. Their enemies conquer them, and the judge delivers them.

• *Ruth:* A story of a foreigner named Ruth who was in the lineage of Christ. Occurred during the time of the judges.

• *1 & 2 Samuel; 1 Kings 1-11:* The United Kingdom. Reign of Saul, David and Solomon, who each ruled the land for 40 years. First Samuel is about the reign of Saul; 2 Samuel is about the reign of David; and 1 Kings 1-11 is about the reign of Solomon.

• *1 Kings 12–2 Kings:* The Divided Kingdom: Israel and Judah. Israel was the northern kingdom for 250 years before being taken over by the Assyrians. Judah was the southern kingdom for 350 years before being taken over by the Babylonians. Israel had 19 rulers; Judah had 20 rulers. The prophets lived during the time of the divided kingdoms, the captivity and the return to Jerusalem.

• *2 Chronicles* gives the more complete account of Judah.

• *Daniel 1-6:* Daniel and Ezekiel were prophets during the Babylonian captivity. Daniel gives the history of the captivity in Daniel 1-6. The Persians took the Babylonians captive, thus receiving the Jews. The Persian king, Cyrus, freed the Jews to go home and back to Jerusalem.

• *Esther, Ezra, Nehemiah:* Ezra and Nehemiah tell of the return to Canaan by the Jews. Zerubbabel, Ezra and Nehemiah led groups back home. Zerubbabel rebuilt the temple, Ezra taught the people, and Nehemiah rebuilt the walls. Esther lived during the time of the Persians.

• *Haggai, Zechariah, Malachi:* They were three prophets who prophesied after the return to Jerusalem.

• *Job:* Many believe that Job was a patriarch who lived during the time of Genesis.

• *Psalms:* This is a book of songs and poems.

• *Proverbs:* This is a book of wise sayings, not a book of absolutes. Some people make the mistake of trying to make every phrase an absolute truth. For example: Solomon said, "He who finds a wife finds a good thing" (Proverbs 18:22). This is a wise saying but not an absolute.

• *Ecclesiastes:* This is a book where Solomon describes his search for happiness and what is worthwhile in life.

• *Song of Solomon:* This is a love song written by Solomon about the love between one woman and one man. It is poetry.

• *All other prophets* fit into the period of the divided kingdom.

When reading the Old Testament, one might want to read the books in the order as they are given here to get the story. Then go back and read the prophets. Once you have built your foundation, Old Testament study is much easier.

Activities

1. Are you one of those people who would like to study the Bible but don't know where to begin? Do you know a new Christian who feels like this? Where would you tell her to begin?

2. Look up the scriptures listed below, and write down what they have to do with studying the Bible.
   2 Timothy 2:15 (KJV)   Matthew 28:19-20
   2 Timothy 3:16-17   Jeremiah 36:2-8
   Revelation 22:18-19   Deuteronomy 6:6-9
   Psalm 119:9, 11, 40, 44-50, 98-105

3. Answer these questions using the reference book listed with each question. If you do not have some of these reference

books, check with your church library, your preacher or even a local library.

   A. Where is the quote "The gift of God is eternal life" found? (a concordance)

   B. Who was Chushanrishathaim? (a Bible dictionary)

   C. Where is Mount Gilboa located? (an atlas)

   D. Find scriptures about adultery. (a concordance)

   E. Who was Judith? (a Bible dictionary)

   F. Discover some facts about and the location of Bethany. (an atlas)

4. These exercises are to help you experience the different styles of learning.

   A. Study about Paul's trip to Rome by reading the story from Acts 27-28.

   B. Trace Paul's journey on a map. (kinesthetic learner)

   C. If available, watch the story from the *Visual Bible* or find pictures that depict the story. (visual learners)

   D. Pair up with another student and discuss the story together. (auditory learner)

   E. Using a blank map, trace Paul's journey to Rome and write by each place what happened along the journey. (visual and kinesthetic learners)

   F. Make character cards on 3-by-5 cards by writing the name of the character studied on the front and who the character is on the back. Make a card for each character in this story. (kinesthetic learner)

   G. Write lessons that can by learned from this story and share your discoveries with the class. (all learners)

   H. After the study is completed, share with the class which activity you enjoyed the most and why. This might give some an insight into how each person in the group learns.

5. Select a passage or chapter(s) in the Bible and follow this outline to study the text of the Bible. Try Philippians 4 to begin.
   A. Pray for wisdom.
   B. Lay aside presuppositions.
   C. Let the verses speak to you.
   D. Ask: Who? What? Why? When? Where? How? Author? Purpose? Summaries? Conclusions? Context? (setting)
   E. Mark key passages in the Bible.
   F. Make application to your life.
   G. Journal (write about what you read).

6. With one or two more students, discuss the information about the Old Testament and New Testament books.

7. Share with the class how you study the Bible.

8. Share with the class which tools you use in studying the Bible.

9. Conduct research in a Bible dictionary or other help books on several subjects. Suggestions include: Solomon's temple, Herod's temple, city of Jerusalem, or city of Ephesus. Share what you learned with the class.

10. Study the book of Philemon (one chapter) for one week. Share with the class how you studied and what you discovered from the study.

11. Mark in your Bible. Make neat notes. A beginner should have a personal Bible with which she becomes very familiar.

Chapter 4

Fellowship

Melissa Lester

"Be devoted to one another in brotherly love; give preference to one another in honor; not lagging behind in diligence, fervent in spirit, serving the Lord; rejoicing in hope, persevering in tribulation, devoted to prayer, contributing to the needs of the saints, practicing hospitality" (Romans 12:10-13 NASB).

God never intended for the Christian walk to be a life of solitude. Scripture tells us that as Christians we are part of the Lord's body. We are His children and fellow heirs in His kingdom. So what would He have us do with one another? Quite simply, He urges us to join hands, to open our hearts, and to enjoy the journey together.

Ecclesiastes 4:10 reminds us that two are better than one because "if either of them falls, the one will lift up his companion" (NASB). Our Christian friends bring light when the path grows dim and laughter when the road is hard. They draw us back to the path when we stray. When we fall, they lift us up.

Our desire for spiritual companionship – especially with our sisters in Christ – is innate. We need each other. Our fellowship can help us get to heaven. When we consider the lasting significance of our relationships, we realize our friendships are worth exploring. How can we build relationships that will last? A look at Romans 12:10-13 will help us find some answers.

"Be Devoted to One Another"

True fellowship is rooted in love. Worldly friendships are really quite fragile. Relationships of convenience may spring up quickly between people who share common interests, but these friendships easily wither when circumstances change. As Christians, we can expect more. We are not linked to each other by superficial bonds; our unity is found in eternal truths.

Our focus on God gives us a level of fellowship that cannot be found in the world. Colossians 3:14 tells us to "put on love, which is the perfect bond of unity" (NASB). The first seeds are planted when we determine within ourselves to love our fellow Christians. True love is a decision.

The Lord commands us to love each other. Romans 12:10 urges, "Be devoted to one another in brotherly love" (NASB). Love takes commitment, and it also involves some emotional risks. First, we must desire to love each other. Opening our hearts to fellowship means reaching out to others and allowing ourselves to be vulnerable. Second, we must be dedicated – willing to invest time and emotional resources to nurture our relationships. Third, we must be devoted. We are to love our Christian family with the unconditional love described in the Bible. Agape love unselfishly seeks the good of another person above self. Unconditional love is a decision that will help us forgive wrongs and look for the best in each other.

• *Love Must Be Expressed.* Encouraging words are gifts we should give liberally to our loved ones. A familiar quote from George W. Childs reminds us,

> Do not keep the alabaster box of your love and friendship sealed up until your friends are dead. Fill their lives with sweetness. Speak approving, cheering words while their ears can hear them, and while their hearts

can be thrilled and made happier. The kind things you mean to say before they are gone, say before they go.

Proverbs 25:11 says this more concisely: "A word aptly spoken is like apples of gold in settings of silver" (NIV). The people in our lives will never know how much they mean to us unless we tell them. A note of encouragement can be saved to read and reread for many years, and spoken words can be tucked into the heart. Words of affection, admiration and appreciation help us feel more secure in our relationships.

Love that is expressed also encourages us to be our best selves. As adults, we still need encouragement and praise. When we express our love to others, we encourage them to grow into the fullness of what God would have them be.

• *Love Must Be Demonstrated.* It is not enough for us to tell fellow Christians we love each other; that commitment must be demonstrated. Our actions show our loved ones what words fail to express. Throughout this chapter, we will explore ways we build fellowship through demonstrating love for our Christian family. Individually and as a body, we put love into action as we fulfill our charge in Romans 12:10-13.

The Bible gives us a beautiful example of love in the enduring friendship between Naomi and Ruth. Despite tremendous hardship and differences in age, culture and religious history, these two unlikely women cultivated a beautiful relationship. Today their friendship endures as it inspires us through the Bible. We see in Naomi and Ruth that with God as the focus, even lost love can give way to lasting love. Their example shows us the fellowship we can enjoy when we begin with love.

"Give Preference to One Another in Honor"

Beyond loving one another, Paul tells us in Romans 12:10 that our devotion will be expressed as we prefer one another in honor. This phrase mentions two gifts we are to give our brothers and sisters in Christ: honor and preference. The two go hand-in-hand in helping us cultivate fellowship.

• *Honor.* In *The Gift of Honor*, John Trent and Gary Smalley say,

"Honor is a decision we make to place high value, worth and importance on another person by viewing him or her as a priceless gift and granting him or her a position in our lives worthy of great respect; and love involves putting that decision into action." [1]

When we think about honor, concepts such as moral integrity, high esteem or recognition of accomplishment probably come to mind. We should hold fellow Christians in high esteem. God has adopted us into His family as "fellow heirs" in His kingdom (Romans 8:17; Ephesians 3:6). When women first meet, our relationships are already on a whole new level because of our shared focus on Christ. We are a family bound by the blood of the cross.

When we give fellow Christians a high position in our lives, we attach high value to them. Value is an intrinsic quality that is difficult to quantify because it is subjective. But the amount of value you attach to something correlates to the care you give it.

It is interesting to watch TV programs in which viewers let experts evaluate their antiques. Often the hopeful homeowners have scoured their attics in search of forgotten treasure. The object brought in for appraisal was likely cast aside years ago with no thought to the damage it might sustain from weather and dust. Isn't it amazing that in one moment such an object can go from a discarded piece of junk to a rare and priceless antique? Depending on the appraisal, the care afforded to the object may change dramatically because its value may rise in its owner's eyes.

The Bible gives us a clear picture – or appraisal – of our value in God's eyes. Genesis 1:26-28 tells us that God created man and blessed him. Zephaniah 3:17 expresses His delight over His children: "Jehovah thy God is in the midst of thee, a mighty one who will save; he will rejoice over thee with joy; he will rest in his love; he will joy over thee with singing" (ASV). First Corinthians 6:20 and 7:23 tell us we were bought with a price, and Ephesians 2:4-7 tells us in beautiful detail how much God cares for us:

> [B]ut God, being rich in mercy, for his great love wherewith he loved us, even when we were dead through

our trespasses, made us alive together with Christ (by grace have ye been saved), and raised us up with him, and made us to sit with him in the heavenly (places), in Christ Jesus: that in the ages to come he might show the exceeding riches of his grace in kindness toward us in Christ Jesus. (ASV)

The Bible is indeed the greatest love story ever told. Realizing how much God values each precious soul He has created should help us value each other more.

We are to care for our fellow Christians as we would for our own bodies. Although we may sometimes feel displeased with certain aspects of our bodies, ultimately most of us do value our bodies. First Corinthians 12:18 reminds us, "But now God has placed the members, each one of them, in the body, just as He desired" (NASB). Isn't it amazing to realize that the God who placed the stars in the heavens has set each of us in His body? This verse reminds us that He lovingly positioned us with forethought and care. As we consider these things, we realize that despite their imperfections, our brothers and sisters in Christ are priceless gifts.

• *Preference.* When we honor women by giving them high value and a high position in our lives, preferring one another will be the natural result. Our sisters in Christ will be our dearest friends, and some of our greatest joys will be found in our times together. The seeds of fellowship will be laid as we gather to worship and study God's Word. As we share prayers and class discussion, we will find security in our common bond. We will seek opportunities to help our friendships grow by organizing "family" activities – a care group potluck, ladies retreat or singles game night.

Ultimately our relationships will flourish when we allow our friendships, particularly with our sisters in Christ, to move beyond the church building and into our lives. As we strive to be godly daughters, wives and mothers, we will draw support and understanding through our contact with each other during the week. We will eagerly await planned outings to grab a cup of coffee, get some exercise or tackle a home improvement project together. And as we grow closer, we will find that our lives intersect more and more.

Amazingly, these bonds of fellowship can be found in the church in people we barely even know. In her *Christian Woman* article "Modern-Day Macedonians," author Karen Pruitt related how Christians eased her daughter Hillary's transition into a new community. When the Pruitts made the seven-hour journey to Hillary's new job at the Mount Dora, Fla., Christian Home and Bible School, co-workers went out of their way to help Hillary feel at home. Although preparing to go out of town themselves, one couple took the Pruitts to lunch and gave them a tour of the town and school.

Another couple researched housing possibilities and took the Pruitts to see several areas. When the best option turned out to be a rental house that would not be ready for a couple of weeks, this couple insisted that Hillary move in with them until the house was complete. At the end of the visit, Hillary planned to take her parents to the airport alone, but her new Mount Dora co-workers stayed on the phone until they found someone who could accompany Hillary on the hour-long drive.

"When we left, we exchanged hugs with everyone in the school office," Pruitt wrote. "We felt truly loved by family members we had never met before but knew we had all over the world. We were moving our daughter away from home, but we felt good. We were leaving her with family."[2]

"Serving the Lord"

Service is an important aspect of our relationship with God. It also enhances our relationships with fellow Christians, as Romans 12:11 attests. This verse reminds us that Christians should not be "lagging behind in diligence" but "fervent in spirit, serving the Lord" (NASB). Fellowship manifests itself as we serve in two ways.

• *Serving Side-by-Side.* First we serve shoulder-to-shoulder in the kingdom. As we busy ourselves teaching, visiting and ministering in myriad ways, working together will strengthen our fellowship. Laughter and conversation flow when women work together. Enthusiasm grows as we encourage each other in the mission field. Friendships blossom as we serve God together.

We can look to Luke 10:38-42 to see how Mary and Martha could have benefited from fellowship. In this familiar story, Jesus and His followers visited the sisters' home. As Mary sat at Jesus' feet, Martha was left to do the serving alone. Irritation with her sister grew until finally Martha broke. "Lord, do You not care that my sister has left me to do all the serving alone? Then tell her to help me" (v. 40 NASB). Jesus responded in verses 41-42, "Martha, Martha, you are worried and bothered about so many things; but only one thing is necessary, for Mary has chosen the good part, which shall not be taken away from her" (NASB).

In her book *Having a Mary Heart in a Martha World*, Joanna Weaver contrasts the kitchen service Martha offered with the living room intimacy Mary enjoyed. Weaver acknowledges,

> Because we are His children, kitchen service will be the natural result of living room intimacy with God. Like Jesus, we must be about our Father's business. The closer we draw to the heart of the Father, the more we see His heart for the world. And so we serve, we minister and we love, knowing that when we do it to "the least of these," we have done it unto Him. [3]

However, she cautions women against getting caught in the performance trap of trying to do it all. She uses the analogy of putting the cart before the horse when we put work before worship. "The cart is important; so is the horse," she says. "But the horse must come first, or we end up pulling the cart ourselves." [4]

I can't help wondering how the sisters' encounter with Jesus might have been different if they had approached the visit together. As they busied themselves in the kitchen, perhaps they could have talked about questions they wanted to ask the Teacher. Martha's "to do" nature could have balanced Mary's "to be" nature as they combined practical tasks with prayer and praise.

Perhaps in the end both sisters would have been eager to welcome Jesus into their home – and their hearts. And as sisters in Christ, isn't our greatest responsibility to help each other prepare to meet our Lord?

• *Serving Each Other.* We also grow in fellowship as we serve each other. As women, most of us are caretakers. At once we may find ourselves tending to the needs of our husbands, children, grandchildren and even our parents. We nurture co-workers and help shoulder the burdens of friends. We are sometimes moved to act on behalf of strangers in need. So I wonder, who takes care of the caretakers? I believe the natural choice is other women. We can relate to each other's struggles with empathy and understanding.

Galatians 5:14 tells us, "For the whole Law is fulfilled in one word, in the statement, 'You shall love your neighbor as yourself'" (NASB). We often look at this passage in terms of its broad application to treat others as we would like to be treated. But I believe we can also make very specific application of this verse, in that our unique life experiences better prepare us to serve those who follow in our footsteps. Through our service, we can brighten their path.

One of my favorite stories is "The Love Squad" by Virelle Kidder. In this touching essay, Kidder shares the comfort she received during a family crisis. After a week-long hospital stay at the bedside of a sick child, her heart sank to find cars in the driveway when she returned home. When she dragged herself inside, her closest friends were surprised to see her. "We weren't expecting you for another hour! We thought we'd be long gone before you got home," Judie explained with a hug.[5] Kidder was astonished to discover the work her friends had done. The women had cleaned house, washed and ironed laundry, changed sheets and placed flowers and little gifts throughout her home. The table was set with dinner, with more meals in the freezer. After her friends left, Kidder sobbed as she wandered through the house. Finally, she reveals, "In the living room, I found a note under a vase filled with peonies. I was to have come home and found it as their only identity: 'The Love Squad was here.' And I knew that God had everything under control." [6]

"Rejoicing in Hope, Persevering in Tribulation"

Before my son Carson was even 2 years old, he would burst into the room with his hands over his head to exclaim, "I did it!" Whether he had built a great tower of blocks or mastered a new game, each new achievement was an occasion to celebrate. His daddy and I were eager to share his happiness with every discovery. Our little boy would beam with pride as we hugged and cheered, because even as a toddler, Carson had learned the important lesson that joy is amplified when it is shared.

Lord Byron wrote, "All who joy would win/Must share it, – happiness was born a twin." The happiest times in our lives are more special when they are shared. Perhaps that's why Paul urges us in Romans 12:12 to rejoice in hope. On an individual basis, fellowship grows as we reach out to our brothers and sisters in good times. Making a phone call to congratulate someone on a promotion takes little time but shows our support. Sending a card to encourage a young person's school achievement – perhaps including a newspaper clipping citing their accomplishment – can leave a lasting impression. Visiting the hospital or delivering a home-cooked meal to welcome a baby means so much to new parents. Even something as simple as sharing a grandmother's pride over her grandchild's latest pictures communicates that we rejoice with our sister in Christ.

As a church family, we mark milestones such as births, graduations, weddings and anniversaries with celebration. In our large congregation, we have many opportunities to celebrate. In particular, we have a steady stream of weddings and births. To ensure that no one's celebration is overlooked, one woman has taken the initiative to organize a "Teas and Showers Notebook." When news begins to circulate about a new engagement or pregnancy, members are asked to let Sara know. She then contacts the bride- or mother-to-be and prepares a page including the wedding or due date, gift registry and other pertinent details.

Hostesses sign up to plan a shower, and ladies gather on a Sunday afternoon to share in the joy of our sister in Christ. As a special gift at baby showers, the mother-to-be is presented a one-of-a-kind baby quilt embroidered by special friends in the congregation. Joy is amplified when we rejoice with those who rejoice.

The flip side of the coin is that as Christians, we share each other's sorrows. Romans 12:12 tells us to persevere in tribulation. The story is told of a mother who watched her little boy cross the street to visit a neighbor who had recently lost his wife. The man sat on his front porch in his rocking chair, obviously broken with grief. The woman watched through her window as her son climbed into the widower's lap. When her son returned a while later, she asked him what he had said. "Nothing," the little one replied. "I just helped him cry."

In the face of tragedy, we often feel ill-equipped to offer comfort. What can we say to ease the suffering of someone who has lost a loved one? What can we do for someone who has lost a job or been betrayed by a spouse? Sometimes we keep our distance from those who are suffering because we just don't know what to do. Benjamin Jowett gently prods us to remain steadfast: "When there is a temper of sympathy in us it hardly matters whether we say little or much to others in company; the friendly smile, the ready attention, the kind pressure of a hand, is enough to make us understood by them, and to make all things known to us." [7] Acts of thoughtfulness demonstrate our care, but often it is our steady presence during times of trouble that communicates more than anything we could say or do.

If we desire to share the joys and sorrows of others – especially our sisters in Christ – our challenge as Christian women is that we must be alert. It is so easy to become consumed with our own schedules, responsibilities and trials, but we must remain interested and involved in the lives of others.

When we experience fellowship through times of joy and sorrow, the road we travel will be made easier. We will smile as we recollect joyful celebrations. As time passes, painful wounds will heal, and we will be left with bittersweet memories. Looking back to those moments will be like rereading a love story, as we remember the kindnesses of our Christian family.

"Devoted to Prayer"

Romans 12:12 reminds us that we are to be women of prayer. Through prayer we open our hearts to God and allow His peace to fill us. He has given us an amazing opportunity to come before His throne. Not only does he allow us to come; He implores us to come. "Come unto me, all ye that labor and are heavy laden, and I will give you rest," Jesus soothes in Matthew 11:28 (ASV). Through prayer we can take our burdens to God and leave them at His feet.

Prayer draws us closer to the heart of our Father, and it also strengthens our bonds with each other. Fellowship grows as we pray for each other. It is difficult to feel distant from someone you pray for regularly. If you pray for a sister in Christ, compassion grows as you consider her life and its unique challenges, responsibilities and heartbreaks. James 5:16 reminds us that God heeds the prayers of the righteous. I have taken part in classes or retreats where each participant committed to pray for another in the group. Knowing that a sister in Christ regularly approached the throne of God with my name on her heart gave me great comfort.

We also grow through praying together as sisters in Christ. Scripture tells us that Lydia had a custom of praying at the riverside with other women (Acts 16:13-14). It was during this regular prayer time that her heart was opened to heed the words spoken by Paul. When our Wednesday night ladies Bible class was suspended for the summer, several in the group decided to continue meeting in an unused classroom to pray. The class became a highlight of the week for all because hearts were opened when we prayed together.

Along with praying with each other publicly, our fellowship grows as we pray with each other privately. We can do this one-on-one in our friendships with sisters in Christ. James 5:16 urges us, "Confess therefore your sins one to another, and pray one for another, that ye may be healed" (ASV). Sharing our struggles with a trusted friend can strengthen our resolve to do better, and praying together will help us feel a greater sense of accountability.

It means so much to have Christian sisters with whom we can pray. When we find ourselves so weak physically, emotionally or spiritually that we don't even have the strength to pray, how blessed we are to have friends who will pick us up and carry us to the Lord.

"Contributing to the Needs of the Saints"

We have been abundantly blessed as Christians, and we please God when we share the gifts He has given us. Romans 12:13 reminds us to contribute to the needs of the saints. When we think about giving to meet the needs of the saints, our material blessings are probably the first that come to mind. Our blessings bring responsibility, as 1 John 3:17 reminds us: "But whoever has the world's goods, and sees his brother in need and closes his heart against him, how does the love of God abide in him?" (NASB). When a brother or sister suffers, we have opportunity to come together as the family of God to help meet those needs. And if we give, God will take care of us.

Another gift we give each other is wisdom. Especially as sisters in Christ, we have so much to learn from each other. Titus 2:3-5 is a familiar passage that instructs older women to encourage the younger women. This flow of knowledge happens in ladies Bible classes, but it also passes naturally when we cultivate relationships with women of different ages. If we reach out to women of many different backgrounds, their friendships will enrich our lives. After all, our differences cannot be greater than the bond that unites us as Christians.

To promote fellowship, what we need to share most is our lives. Joseph Fort Newton urges, "Share your life, and find the finest joy man can know. Do not be stingy with your heart. Get out of yourself into the lives of others, and new life will flow into you – share and share alike." What our sisters in Christ need most from us is our friendship. Gifts of time, interest, affection and thoughtfulness will promote fellowship. Galatians 6:10 urges, "So then, while we have opportunity, let us do good to all people, and especially to those who are of the household of the faith" (NASB). The time we have on earth is a gift from God, and sharing it with our Christian family will make every moment count.

"Practicing Hospitality"

God desires that we practice hospitality as a church body because we will grow in our love for each other as a result. Reading Acts 2:41-47, we can sense the enthusiasm of the early Christians and their sincere desire to be together. Verse 42 reads, "They were continually devoting themselves to the apostles' teaching and to fellowship, to the breaking of bread and to prayer" (NASB). The fellowship shared by these early Christians grew their faith and the kingdom as well.

A commitment to hospitality will strengthen our relationships with other Christians because fellowship grows as our lives become more connected. One of my favorite authors, Emilie Barnes, shared this bit of wisdom about hospitality: "Hospitality is so much more than entertaining – so much more than menus and decorating and putting on a show. To me, it means organizing my life in such a way that there's always room for one more, always an extra place at the table or an extra pillow and blanket, always a welcome for those who need a listening ear. It means setting aside time for planned fellowship and setting aside lesser priorities for impromptu gatherings."[8] Many of us miss opportunities for fellowship because we set such lofty goals that we give up before we even begin. Letting go of perfectionism will help us find greater joy in hospitality.

If we are blessed to have a home, welcoming people into it will help them learn more about us. No matter what kind of dwelling we live in, we can extend friendship and hospitality. In her column "A Matter of Taste," Bernie Arnold introduced *Christian Woman* readers to a hostess who made the most of her small space. When Mary Binkley Williams and her late husband downsized from the spacious home where they had raised five children to a small condo, she found new ways to entertain. Undeterred by the lack of room for a large dining table, Williams welcomed guests with lovely basket lunches for a picnic in the parlor. She filled each guest's basket with tasty finger foods, and added pretty details with flowers, tissue paper and ribbon. Creativity allowed Williams to seek new ways to show hospitality.[9]

Although a certain intimacy is achieved by entertaining in the home, opportunities abound for hospitality outside the home. Being hospitable might mean visiting a shut-in, calling someone who is facing a personal struggle, or taking a special interest in visitors at church. A trip to a tea room might provide a perfect opportunity to bond with a new sister in Christ, or an afternoon play date at the zoo might provide fun and fellowship for young mothers.

If you find that your definition of hospitality makes it seem impossible for you to reach out to others, change your definition! Different stages of life offer unique opportunities and challenges, so keeping an open mind will help you reach out to others whatever your circumstances. Joe and I were so excited when we bought our first house. Our little house couldn't accommodate large groups, so we made a regular practice of inviting one or two couples at a time for Sunday lunch. I had a few standard menus I had mastered, so we served the same lunch to about half of our congregation. Sometimes we would prepare extra food so that we could include visitors to our services.

As our circumstances changed, it was more difficult to entertain weekly, but we found ways to accommodate larger groups. I discovered that I really enjoy planning ladies events. I have found women to be so appreciative of the time and care you put into serving them. Many of my fondest memories are from the girls nights, luncheons and afternoon teas we have shared.

At its core, hospitality is not so much about opening your home as it is about opening your heart. In fact, the best hostess is simply a friend – someone who is willing to share her life and time. With empathy and understanding, she is always willing to listen and quick to offer encouragement. Proverbs 27:9 says, "Oil and perfume make the heart glad, So a man's counsel is sweet to his friend." Ultimately hospitality is less about meeting people's physical needs and more about meeting their spiritual and emotional needs. When we share our lives with other Christians, along the way we will experience companionship, laughter and understanding.

Fellowship Found

Romans 12:10-13 gives us so many insights into cultivating relationships within our Christian family. As we seek fellowship, we begin with devotion to each other. In order to last, our love for each other must be committed, expressed and demonstrated. Our relationships should be characterized by honor. As we give fellow Christians high value and high position in our lives, preferring one another will come as a natural result. Serving each other and serving side-by-side will deepen our friendships. As we grow closer, we will share joys and sorrows. Through prayer we will draw closer to God and to our Christian family. And with a generous spirit, we will seek to give of ourselves. In doing so, we will find ourselves most blessed. And finally, by practicing hospitality we will invite others into our lives. In our quest for fellowship, we will find ourselves on a heavenward journey that has been immeasurably blessed by the opportunity to travel this road together.

Activities

1. Show a sister in Christ that your love is committed by writing a heartfelt letter of encouragement or surprising her with a thoughtful gesture.

2. Honor someone in your congregation who needs a lift by reaching out in an unexpected way, such as preparing a gift basket or involving her in an activity.

3. Get involved in a new ministry at your congregation. As you serve alongside sisters in Christ, look for unmet needs of oth-

ers within the group. Could you offer baby-sitting to a young mom or a home-cooked meal to someone who works?

4. Find something to celebrate! Plan a party to celebrate the youth group's participation in Bible Bowl, surprise a widow with a birthday cake, or serve as a hostess for a wedding shower.

5. Ease the suffering of a Christian sister by keeping vigil with her during a loved one's surgery.

6. Pray individually for each person in your Bible class. Pray with a friend who confides in you.

7. Plan a lunch date with a Christian sister you admire. Tell her how much you admire her example as a wife, mother or teacher. Seek her advice in this area.

8. Think of a fun theme for an event you could plan, such as a football season barbecue for singles; a New Year's Day brunch for young families; or an afternoon tea for the ladies class. Collect recipes and fun ideas for the event, and exchange completed menus with other class members. (Now pull out the calendar and see who wants to be the first hostess!)

Chapter 5

Outreach

Pamela Stewart

If a woman came to your Sunday morning assembly, and in talking with her it became clear that she had questions about the church, who would answer her questions? Most of the time it would be the preacher. Other times a woman will agree to help teach, but only if her husband will lead the study. This should not be. Christian women are capable of teaching other women. With the right encouragement and the right plan, it can happen. What does the Word of God say about women's responsibility in this area?

Mary Magdalene and several other women had a very important mission. The women were headed to the tomb of Jesus. When they got there, they found grave clothes but no body. Jesus had risen. Then, when they recognized Jesus in the garden, He sent them on a very important mission. He told them to go and tell the other disciples that He had risen from the dead. Jesus could have revealed Himself to anyone for the first time after His resurrection. He could have chosen anyone to take the important message to the disciples, but He chose women (Matthew

28:1-10; Mark 16:1). Doesn't this tell us something about what He expects of us concerning taking His message to the people?

After the Samaritan woman had a long talk with Jesus at the well, she went back into the city of Sychar and told everyone about Him. John says that many people believed because of the testimony of the Samaritan woman (John 4:39). Will it be said of you that many people believed because of your testimony?

Women are not exempt from the Great Commission. Jesus said, "[G]o and make disciples of all nations, baptizing them in the name of the Father and of the Son and of the Holy Spirit, and teaching them to obey everything I have commanded you" (Matthew 28:19-20 NIV). "Go" includes women.

If we are not involved in teaching women, perhaps it is because we have not truly developed a love for the Lord. "For out of the overflow of the heart the mouth speaks" (Matthew 12:34 NIV). We must develop an overflow through study and prayer. The mouth will speak if we love Jesus because then, and only then, will we have an overflow. Women talk about what they love. Our overflow leads us to talk about our children, our grandchildren, our husbands, our jobs and our hobbies. Why, then, would our love for the Lord not lead us to talk about Him? If you were looking at a picture of my granddaughter and you were asked to tell us about her, you would not have much to say because you do not know her. If you were asked to show us a picture of your granddaughter and tell us about her, you would have much to say. Why? It is because you have an overflow. You know her, and you love her. We must know and love Christ. We must develop an overflow in our hearts that will lead us to talk about Him.

Statistics tell us that women want to be involved in spreading the gospel, but they do not want to be the one to do the teaching. They will go with their husbands, be cordial, or keep the children while he studies with someone. They agree to work in the area of hospitality and have people in their homes to help them get acquainted or involved. They love the benevolent ministry and are very good at reaching out to those in need. Some will agree to give a devotional in the ladies Bible class. They work in all kinds of service ministries. They look forward to teaching children. They are serious about raising their own children in the Lord's Way. All these ministries are important, and they help in the Lord's work, but it is also our responsibility to lead women to Christ through studying the Word with them. How will we get this job done? When asked to teach the gospel to someone who is not a Christian, many women feel unprepared. They are afraid they will be asked a question they cannot answer. We must become prepared.

Types of Outreach Lessons

You must prepare yourself. You must read the Word and pray every day. You must ask God to guide you. You must prepare your lessons. You may use lessons that someone else has put together or prepare the lessons personally. Do not be afraid to use "cheat sheets." The points that you want to make, the illustrations, and the questions will all be on the sheet. The lessons presented in this section are simple and to the point. If you decide to use them, you should add to them and make them your own.

• *A Lifeline.* This is a very informal lesson. Draw a line across a paper. Ask the person with whom you are studying to share with you her religious experiences starting with the first experience she can remember. Put her experiences on the line. The purpose for this is so that you can refer back to this lifeline at the end of the lessons if she is confused about what she has obeyed or not obeyed. The second purpose is to get acquainted. Share with her your experiences also. You will start a great relationship on which to build.

• *Seeking God.* This lesson should teach the importance of seeking God and how to seek Him on His terms, not on our own. What are most people seeking today? Money, love, happiness, fun and fame to name a few. The Bible tells us to seek first His kingdom. Look at Bible examples of seekers, such as the Ethiopian (Acts 8:26-40) and the Bereans (Acts 17:11).

• *A Study of Sin.* Do not assume the woman with whom you are studying knows what sin is. Movies and television distort our thinking about sin. List and define all the sins in the lists in Mark 7:20-23; Galatians 5:19-21; Romans 1:18-32; 1 Corinthians 6:9-10; Ephesians 4:31; 5:3; and Colossians 3:5-10. Go over every sin and what it means. Share with her sins that you have struggled with, and let her share with you. Talk about the reason Jesus went to the cross – for us, for our sins.

• *The Cross Study.* This study is to show how much God loves us and to help us gain a deep appreciation for the physical, emotional and spiritual pain Jesus endured in order for us to be reconciled to God (Matthew 26:36–27:54).

• *What Must I Do to Be Saved?* We must have faith (Hebrews 11:6; Romans 10:14-17). We must repent (Acts 2:37-38; Luke 13:3; Acts 3:19). We must confess (Romans 10:9-10; Matthew 10:32-33). We must reenact the death, burial and resurrection of Christ through baptism (1 Corinthians 15:1-4; Romans 6:3-4; Galatians 3:26-27). When we do these things, three great blessings take place: sins are forgiven, the Holy Spirit comes to indwell us, and we are added to the Lord's church.

• *Counting the Cost.* Teach her what it means to be a disciple. A disciple is someone who wants to be just like Jesus. We must have the attitude of Simon Peter. He had fished all night without catching one fish. Yet, when Jesus told him to cast his nets down one more time, Peter did what Jesus told him to do (Luke 5:1-11).

• *A Study of the Church.* This lesson may come before a person obeys the gospel or after. Jesus came to build His church (Matthew 16:15-19). Jesus pleaded before He died that we all be one (John 17:20-23), yet we are very divided. The only way to be one is to follow the plan in the Bible. The Bible tells us how the church is set up, with elders, deacons and members. It gives the name the church should be called. It gives instructions for worship, and it gives directions on how to be a part of it.

• *The Eight Things in Titus 2:3-5.* These are follow-up lessons for after a person has obeyed the gospel. Study and be prepared to teach all the things that women are supposed to teach women listed in this passage of Scripture. Clearly, teaching women these things is women's responsibility. The list is long and can be overwhelming. Yet, it is important to prepare ourselves to teach each of these things. The list includes teaching women:

1. to recognize what is good,
2. to love their husbands,
3. to love their children,
4. to be self-controlled,
5. to be pure,
6. to be busy at home,
7. to be kind, and
8. to be subject to their husbands.

Why should women teach women? "[S]o that no one will malign [dishonor] the word of God" (Titus 2:5 NIV). If we do not teach women to live the life God wants for them and to behave in Christian ways, the Word of God is dishonored. If we allow the men to do our work and teach women the above list, many times the Word is dishonored because it is a tempting situation to put men in the position of teaching women these personal things. If we take over our responsibility in this area, we will alleviate this potential temptation.

Don't ever be afraid to say, "I do not know the answer to that question. I will look into that and give you an answer next week." It is not a disgrace to admit that you do not know everything. In fact, it may cause her to respect you even more because you are humble enough to admit that you do not know it all.

Team Outreach

After you have prepared your lessons to present to women who are not Christians, try to find one other woman who is interested in helping you take the gospel to other women. Assure her that you will do the teaching. Ask her to set aside one night a week to give to this cause. If you go alone, you will be missing a great opportunity to train someone else to do what you are doing.

Three things will take place as you teach: (1) You will teach the lessons to someone who has not heard them. (2) You will train the woman you brought with you to teach the lessons as she hears you teach each week. (3) You, your partner and the new woman will build great relationships that will help her fit into the church. Praying and studying the Word together always builds great relationships.

As time goes on and your partner has heard the lessons over and over, you can divide into two teams. You will find someone else to train. Your partner will find someone else to train. Continue this process until you have many teams. The teams should meet together at least once a month to encourage one another and pray together about the women with whom they are studying. All teams should use the same lessons. Then, if you are not able to go on one of your studies because of sickness or traveling, you can call one of the other teachers to fill in for you. Everyone will know exactly what you have covered in previous lessons and where you are going in the next lesson.

Begin an Outreach Class

Instead of starting with just you and one other person, you can offer a class to the women of your congregation. Advertise the class as one that will help them prepare to teach the gospel. Teach the lessons that will be used to teach new women. The homework for each lesson is to find someone with whom to share the lesson. The person sharing the lesson can tell others that she has homework from the class and that she must share the lesson with someone. She can tell them that she is inexperienced and is in the learning process. This takes away the pressure. Many will agree to help her out by listening. One young woman taught her beautician through this method. It is a good crutch to use until you know your lessons. After you have finished teaching all the lessons, make as many teams as possible for teaching new women.

These methods are certainly not the only methods to use in teaching other women. Years ago we used the Jule Miller filmstrips. Now those lessons, known as *The Visualized Bible Study Series* by Jule Miller and Tex Stevens, are available on video and DVD. You may want to use the *Open Bible Study* along with *Go Ye Into the 21st Century* by Ivan Stewart. For someone who has no understanding of God, Jesus and the church, you might want to study *Evangelism Made Simple.* Whatever method you choose, make sure the women in your teaching ministry all use the same method. You will work together more successfully and encourage each other more effectively if you are all on the same page.

When studying with prospects, never take for granted that they will have a Bible in their home to refer to. For this reason, you may want to purchase some inexpensive Bibles such as New King James Version pew Bibles. When referencing a particular scripture, you can tactfully ask the prospect and your helper to turn to the page number.

Reach Out With Your Talents

Even after a thorough study of all the things women are to teach, and even after a complete set of lessons have been studied, some women will feel they cannot do it. They will tell you it is an unreal expectation to think that all women have the ability to teach other women. We may not believe this to be true, but we must accept it. We must teach them to evangelize through the talents they possess. If they excel at hospitality, help them see that having others in their home can play a role in evangelism. They may work with the women in the teaching teams to help the new women get acquainted with others in the church. If they work in the benevolent room at church, encourage them to put the gospel presentation into every sack of clothing, linens, etc. that goes out. If they enjoy sending cards, ask them to send a greeting to every visitor who comes through your doors. Help every woman develop an evangelistic mindset. Every woman should ask herself the question, "How am I going to help spread the gospel of Jesus Christ?"

The woman who taught me the gospel was our neighbor. Her husband did not want her going to church, and he certainly did not want her taking the neighbor girl. Against all his resistance, she got us both to church every Sunday. She thought she could not do much for the Lord, but her influence goes on and on through many. Perhaps your method of teaching other women is to take a little neighbor girl to church with you.

Open Your Eyes for Prospects

How do you find women with whom to study? This is the easy part. If you prepare yourself, God will send the women. Start praying that God will put a woman in your path who wants to know about Him. Then keep your eyes open for the woman He is sending to you. Talk to the female clerk at the grocery store, your beautician, visitors to church, your child's teacher, and the woman at the ballgame. Simply ask if she would like to go to your congregation. Give her the time of services and ask her if you can provide transportation. If she is not ready to make a commitment, ask when would be a good time to get together to study the Bible.

If a woman visits the church for the first time and you meet her in the foyer, ask her if she has questions about the worship services. She probably will. Ask if you can come by to see her during the next week to get better acquainted and answer her questions through a study of the Bible.

Be brave about asking women if they would like to study the Bible in a small group. The group will consist of you, your partner, and her. As the ones you study with become Christians, they will have friends that they want to reach out to with the gospel. They will need your help. Have them make a list of those they plan to approach about studying. Then, take them with you and your partner when you study with these people. Remember, "God did not give us a spirit of timidity, but a spirit of power, of love and of self-discipline" (2 Timothy 1:7 NIV). If God did not give us the spirit of timidity, who do you think gave it to us?

• Never try to do this on your own power. You will fail. If you think you cannot do it, you are exactly right. But God can do it through you. When we become Christians, the Father sends His Holy Spirit to indwell us (Romans 8:9). The human heart actually becomes the home of God (1 Corinthians 3:16). This means we are not on our own when we teach. Pray to the Father that He will allow His Holy Spirit to work through you to teach the woman the gospel.

• Never try to teach someone else if your heart and your life are not right. Unrepented sin in our own lives will hinder us from being successful teachers. We will never be perfect. There will always be sin in our lives, but it should not be a willful sin that is ruling over us, that we practice, and that we are not willing to give up for God.

All things are to be done from a heart of love for the lost. Our ministry will not be effective if love is not present. God will not bless our ministry if we are doing it out of duty or for social gratification. Jesus spoke of love more than anything else. He said it is one of the identifying marks to show others that we are truly His disciples. He personally preached it and lived it. He asked us to follow His example: "All men will know that you are my disciples, if you love one another" (John 13:35 NIV). Without love, we are only going through the motions. According to the Word, we are as annoying as a "resounding gong or a clanging cymbal" (1 Corinthians 13:1), and we are nothing (v. 2).

When people come through our doors at church, they are not looking for the truth. They do not know there is a truth. They are looking for a place to belong – a place to feel loved and accepted. What are some of the traits of love that we must develop? "Love is patient, love is kind. It does not envy, it does not boast, it is not proud. It is not rude, it is not self-seeking, it is not easily angered, it keeps no record of wrongs. Love does not delight in evil but rejoices in the truth. It always protects, always trusts, always hopes, always perseveres" (1 Corinthians 13:4-7 NIV).

As your ministry grows in number, be sure to take your program to the elders of the congregation. The elders are your overseers. They cannot shepherd if they are not aware of what you are involved in. They need to keep in touch with this ministry.

Will you be the one to step up and start this ministry in your congregation? It may start with you, but it will spread to others, and before long you will have 20 or 30 women in this ministry. Do not neglect them. Meet regularly for prayer and encouragement. One woman approached a woman who worked in an office with her. They had worked side by side for 10 years. She asked if she would study the Bible with her in a small group. The woman agreed. After several studies, the woman became very upset. Her words were, "Do you mean you have known this all along and you have worked by my side for 10 years, and you have never shared this important information with me?" The woman who set up the study was very discouraged at the remark and wanted to quit, but the encouragement and prayers of the teaching group helped her get through a difficult time.

Excuses, Excuses

Right now you are probably thinking of at least a dozen reasons why you cannot do this. You have probably rationalized to the point that you are fooling yourself into thinking they are good excuses. We make excuses out of weakness of our mind and body. Christ will give us wisdom and strength to overcome if we ask Him. We are not the inventor of excuses. People of God in biblical times were just as guilty. When God told Moses He had chosen him to lead His people out of Egypt, Moses made many excuses as to why he could not. Ultimately God's will was accomplished but not without resistance from Moses. Look at the paraphrased dialogue between Moses and God in Exodus 3–4.

God: I am sending you to Pharaoh to bring the Israelites out of Egypt.

Moses: Who am I, that You should send me?

God: I'll be with you.

Moses: Suppose I go to the Israelites and tell them you sent me and they ask who you are?

God: Tell them "I AM."

Moses: What if they won't listen and don't believe me?

God: I'll give you evidences.

Moses: I have never been a good speaker. I am slow.

God: Who gave you your mouth? I will help you and teach you what to say.

Moses: Please send someone else.

God: I am angry. Get your brother Aaron. I will help both of you and teach you what to do.

Have you used some of these same excuses? Have you argued with God about it? Have you asked, "Why should I go?" Are you afraid someone will ask you who God is and you won't be able to tell her? Are you afraid she will not listen? Do you use the excuse that you are not a good speaker? God says, "Who gave you your mouth?" and "I will help you." Yet, we, just as Moses, say, "Please send someone else." Is God angry?

Dealing With Fear

You may be afraid. Don't you think Jesus was afraid when He fell with His face to the ground in the garden of Gethsemane? He was overwhelmed with sorrow at what He was facing. His friends did not understand. They could not even stay awake and hold His hand. Don't you think He was afraid when He was stripped, beaten, spit upon and then led away to be crucified carrying His own cross? And was He afraid when He cried out, "My God, my God, why have you forsaken me?"

By facing your fears and teaching other women the gospel of Christ, you will experience one of the most rewarding things you will ever do. Teaching other women to join you in this effort will be just as fulfilling. If you are a woman who has never led someone to the Lord, you are missing one of the greatest blessings of being a Christian. In fact, the Bible says by being active in sharing our faith, we will have a full understanding of every good thing (Philemon 6). We want an understanding of every good thing, don't we?

Activities

1. Turn to Matthew 28:19-20 and read aloud the verses using three or four translations. Notice how many times the word "you" is used as an indirect subject or the direct object. Does "you" mean only one gender can go and teach?

2. Partner with someone in class. Practice giving each other the "Lifeline" outreach lesson.

3. Brainstorm some methods of reaching out other than those mentioned in "Begin an Outreach Class."

4. What excuses have you used not to go and teach?

Chapter 6

An Overview of the Writing Process

Dwina Willis

Do you remember last Sunday's sermon or the lesson from last Wednesday night's class? Sadly, many of us would have to say that we do not. To present a memorable lesson that will make a difference in people's lives, we have to do more than study the Bible. We have to organize our thoughts and then present them with style. This chapter deals with organizing the material we have gathered as we studied so it can be presented in a clear and memorable way.

Outline

Yes, there's that word "outline" that we hated to see in English class. However, an outline does help us put our thoughts in order so our lesson can progress in a systematic way. Mark Galli and Craig Brian Larson even suggested that working with an outline form forces us to be more creative by channeling our thinking in a specific direction.[1]

An outline should flow according to the following format:

Topic
Scripture
Title

Purpose Statement
Introduction
  I.
     A.
     B.
 II.
     A.
     B.
III.
     A.
     B.
Conclusion

The number of points and sub-points may vary, but the outline form remains the same. More about outlining will be covered in Chapter 7.

Topic, Scripture, Title and Purpose Statement

There are three parts to each lesson: introduction, discussion and conclusion. Before you write any of those, however, a topic, scripture text, title and purpose statement must be determined. It may be that if you are speaking for a ladies day or retreat, you will be assigned some or all of these.

• *Topic.* If you are working on a talk for Lads to Leaders/ Leaderettes, you will have the theme for the year as your springboard for ideas. If you are not given anything, it will be up to you to decide what text will be most relevant to your class. Make sure your subject is not too broad. For instance, a study of friendship could be divided into lessons on friendship with the world, friendship with God, friendship with one another, etc. A narrow study helps you and your listeners focus on the objective you have for the class.

• *Scripture.* Sometimes you may be given a title and then must come up with a text that will be the central idea of the lesson. A good concordance is essential in helping you find those verses.

• *Title.* Sometimes you are given a topic or a text and must come up with a title. A title should reflect the text and be brief, interesting, humorous but not irreverent, and give some insight into what the lesson is about.[2] "Creative Christian Living," Ephesians 2:10; "God's Formula for Success," Joshua 1:6-8; "Make Me a Vessel God Can Use," 2 Timothy 2:20-21; and "Peter Pan Christians," Hebrews 5:12-14 are just a few examples.

• *Purpose Statement.* Writing a purpose statement forces you to focus on the most important thing you want your listeners to get out of your lesson. The statement should be brief and to the point. It should begin with "The students will … ."

For example, the purpose statement for the lesson on "Peter Pan Christians" might state: "The students will understand they should be growing and maturing spiritually." Everything you present in the lesson should help you fulfill the objective stated in your purpose statement.

Discussion

Although the introduction is presented first, it is often written last. The discussion, or main body of the lesson, is usually the first part to be developed. It contains the main points of the lesson and the unfolding of these ideas.

Take the mass of information gathered from your Bible study on your text or topic and isolate the main ideas to be presented. Make sure each idea contributes to the development of the purpose of your lesson. These main points should contain only one idea. If possible, they should be parallel in construction to make them easier to remember. Micah 6:8 is a wonderful example of this. Micah tells us the Lord requires us:

1. "To do justly
2. "To love mercy
3. "To walk humbly with your God."

Another example of parallel construction is found in Ephesians 5. How do we imitate God as commanded in verse 1? We should

1. Walk in love (v. 2)
2. Walk in light (v. 8)
3. Walk in wisdom (v. 15)

Delineating the main points helps the teacher and student remember the lesson. Two or three points may be sufficient to develop the lesson and fulfill your purpose. If you have many more than three, your students will probably not remember them. After you have decided on the main points, arrange them in some type of order – chronological, geographical or logical.

• *Chronological Order.* If you are doing a historical study or a character study, it may be best to arrange the points in chronological order. For example, we see Miriam's life in three short passages in the Old Testament:

1. She talked to Pharaoh's daughter (Exodus 2:7).
2. She led the women in a song of praise (Exodus 15:20-21).
3. She and Aaron spoke against Moses (Numbers 12).

Each of these cameo appearances could be a main point. You might elaborate each of these points to teach how Miriam used her tongue in each instance. Sometimes she used it for good, and sometimes she did not.

• *Geographical Sequence.* Another way to arrange the points is a geographical sequence. A lesson on church history might follow the church beginning in Jerusalem and then spreading to Judea, Samaria, and to the end of the earth (Acts 1:8). A lesson on Paul's missionary journeys would work well with a geographical sequence. Jesus' last days could also follow this sequence. One could trace His steps from the Upper Room to the Garden of Gethsemane to Caiaphas to Pilate's Hall to the cross to the tomb (Matthew 26-27).

• *Logical Order.* Most lessons will use some sort of logical order. Jesus, the Master Teacher, used all of these as He taught the people of His day. Types of logical orders include, but are not limited to:

- Importance or climax – from least important point to most important (Mark 13:5-37)
- General to specific – Begin with broad generalizations and proceed to specific examples, deductive reasoning (Matthew 5:21-24).
- Specific to general – Give examples that lead to a general conclusion, inductive reasoning (Matthew 6:25-34).
- Cause to effect – Name a cause, and trace its consequences (Matthew 21:21-22).
- Effect to cause – Begin with the results or effect and discover the probable cause (Mark 7:9-13).
- Question and answer – Questions are the main points, and answers are the sub-points. (Luke 6:32-49; Matthew 25:31-46).
- Comparison and contrast – Comparisons show likenesses; contrasts show differences (Matthew 5:14-16; 7:24-27).
- Analogy – Show the relation between two things to clarify their meaning (John 15:1-8).
- Definition – Help the listener understand the meaning of a word used in a particular context (Matthew 5:21-22).
- Familiarity – Use something the audience knows to explain the unknown (Matthew 13).
- Problem and solution – A problem is discussed by offering possible solutions (Luke 10:25-37).[3]

Different lessons will require different ways of presenting the material. For example, in a lesson on abstinence to teenage girls, a cause to effect approach might work best. Some of the problems connected with sexual promiscuity might be given. It is sinful, and it is irresponsible (risking unwanted pregnancy and sexually transmitted disease). A lesson on love might define some of the Greek or Hebrew words translated as "love" in our English Bible to help define the concept of love. Choose the type of progression best suited to the lesson you are delivering. If you are teaching a class on a weekly basis, different types of progression on different weeks might help keep the students' attention.

Developing Main Points

As you enlarge your outline to develop your main points, the supporting material should provide any or all of the following:

• *Clarification.* Do not assume everyone understands what you mean. Concepts or abstract terms such as "grace" and "faith," the meaning of which older Christians take for granted, may need to be defined or explained to non-Christians or to those young in the faith. Jesus did this for the Samaritan woman (John 4). Children need concrete examples of these abstract concepts too. You may also be surprised how ignorant many people are of the Bible. A biblical character or event that may be very familiar to you may be new to your listeners. You may need to tell the story connected to the passage you are using.

• *Reinforcement.* This strengthens the point of agreement in a more vivid way and helps the listener put the concept into action. This may answer the question, "How does this concept impact my life?" Jesus reinforced the lawyer's understanding of what was necessary to inherit eternal life by telling the story of the good Samaritan. Jesus then told the lawyer to "go and do likewise" (Luke 10:25-37).

• *Proof.* Any point the students do not believe must be proved (1 Thessalonians 5:21). This can be done in several ways. First, reliable facts and figures can help to make your point. Make sure the sources are accurate. You will lose credibility if your statistics are inaccurate or out of date. Second, specific examples and illustrations from the Bible, history, current events or personal experience can strengthen your position. Third, authoritative testimony can prove a point. Jesus chose this when He was tempted, using the authority of the Scriptures (Matthew 4:4). Finally, a comparison can help connect the known to the unknown. In Matthew 13, Jesus compared the kingdom of heaven to a mustard seed, leaven, a treasure, etc.[4]

The Introduction

The audience may be won or lost by the way you begin your lesson. The purpose of an introduction is to arouse the interest of your listeners, to establish the purpose of the lesson, and/or to show the relevancy of this topic in their lives.

To catch a fish, you must use the correct bait. There must be something on the hook to make the fish want to bite. Once the fish bites, you have to reel it in and get it into the net. The same principle is true in teaching a group of girls or women. If you want them to concentrate on the main points in your talk, you must use the right lure at the beginning of the lesson to "hook" their attention and "reel" them into the discussion of your lesson. Then you can present your main points and finish the lesson with a forceful conclusion.

Types of Introductions

Just as a fisherman would use different lures for different fish, teachers use different types of introductions. What you use depends on the audience, the topic, and the setting. Here are some suggestions for different types of introductions.

• *Reading or quoting the text.* This is especially helpful if the text relates to something the listeners are currently dealing with in their lives.

• *A quotation or poem.* Begin a lesson from Luke 16:13 with this quote from an unknown author: "Money is a wonderful servant, but it is a terrible god."

• *Background information.* Use Bible customs or geography that relate to and enhance your lesson – especially if they are interesting and not widely known.

• *An illustration or story.* This can be from history, current events, literature, personal experience, etc.

• *An open-ended, thought-provoking question.* The question from Matthew 16:26 – "For what is a man profited, if he shall gain the whole world, and lose his own soul? or what will a man give in exchange for his soul?" (NIV) – might be used to introduce a lesson on priorities.

• *A life situation.* This story might come from your own life or the life of another. Be a people-watcher. Make sure the story relates to your purpose.

• *Object lesson.* Minister Ben Flatt began a devotional talk by pulling an onion out of a paper bag. He asked the students to look at his "rose." He then began to list sins that our culture has renamed, for example homosexuality is an alternate lifestyle, cursing is colorful speech, adultery is an affair, etc. He concluded with the comment that if those things were not sins, his onion was a "rose."

• *Seeming contradiction or paradox.* A good example of this is found in Matthew 16:25: "For whoever desires to save his life will lose it, and whoever loses his life for My sake will find it."

• *Bible story.* People never tire of hearing familiar Bible stories. Others may have never heard the story. Practice your storytelling skills.

• *Facts or statistics.* Make sure your facts are current and from a reliable source. Not all Internet sites are reliable.

• *Definition.* This is helpful when a word in the lesson is unfamiliar or may have numerous meanings. The different dimensions of love would be one example. However, don't start your lesson by quoting the definition from a dictionary.

• *Movies, children's books or songs.* An excerpt from a Dr. Seuss book would catch someone's attention. A reference to a current or classic movie, such as *It's a Wonderful Life,* or a song would also catch the attention of an audience.

These are just a few suggestions. Knowing the purpose of the lesson will help you choose something that will have your audience anticipating the main part of your lesson.

Qualities of an Introduction

An introduction should be brief. You are preparing your listeners for the main body of the lesson. To do this, avoid unnecessary jokes, elaborate thanks, greetings or apologies. You need to spend the majority of the time allotted in teaching.

Second, the introduction should also be easy to understand. Jesus used simple words when He taught. You do not need to impress your audience with your vocabulary or expertise in some area.

Third, the introduction should relate to the audience. This is more challenging when your listeners are diverse in age or when you are a guest speaker and do not know the audience. When this is the case, you may want to use a story or poem that is universal in its appeal.

One of the best introductions I ever heard was one Layne Keele, at the time a student at Freed-Hardeman University, presented in chapel. He told the audience he was going to give them the secret to his academic successes in two words.

> Those two words are not "hard work." It's not "positive attitude." The two words that spell success at FHU – "Courier New." You see, Courier New is a computer font that lets me put the least effort in, and get the most results out.

The students loved getting the secret to an easy way to succeed in classes. They were hanging on his every word. Then Layne reminded them of a man in Mark 10:17-22 who, Layne said, "wanted to take the Courier New approach to his spiritual life." You could have heard a pin drop in that huge auditorium. Layne's introduction was not long. It was simple to understand, and it related to the students' lives at that time.

Make sure the introduction helps to fulfill the purpose of your lesson as well as captures the interest of your audience. You want the listeners to anticipate what is coming in the discussion. A few sentences to transition into the main points will help.

Transitions

Just as a relay team needs a smooth hand-off when the baton is passed from one runner to another, a transition is needed when moving from one main point to another. It lets the audience know the speaker is moving to the next area of discussion. It may also spark an interest for what is to follow.

A transition may contain a key word from a previous point or from the purpose statement. It may contain connective words and phrases such as "because," "then," "therefore," "but," "in addition," etc. It may be a question connecting the two points. Hebrews 12:1-2 is a great example of a transition from the "Faith Hall of Fame" to the application for the readers of the book:

> Therefore we also, since we are surrounded by so great a cloud of witnesses, let us lay aside every weight, and the sin which so easily ensnares us, and let us run with endurance the race that is set before us, looking unto Jesus, the author and finisher of our faith.

The Conclusion

James Braga wrote that the conclusion is "the climax of the whole lesson" in which a speaker's one aim "reaches its goal in the form of a forceful impression."[5] J.J. Turner compared the conclusion of a lesson to "a lawyer's final address to the jury before it goes out to deliberate on a verdict. A good lawyer knows that he may win or lose a case with his concluding remarks."[6] You may or may not get the desired response from the listeners based on the strength of your conclusion.

Types of Conclusions

• *Summary.* A conclusion can summarize what has been said. If biblical knowledge is the aim of your lesson, this may be the best type of conclusion. Lora Laycook used to say in her teacher training classes, that the "Three R's" of learning were "Repetition, repetition and repetition." A summary in your conclusion reinforces the information presented in the lesson.

• *Application.* The conclusion of a lesson may also make an application to the listeners' lives. Most Bible students want to know more than Bible facts. They want to know how this information impacts them today. We do not want our students to be like trained seals that can spout lots of Bible facts but do not exhibit these Bible principles in their lives.

• *Motivational.* The conclusion may also appeal to the emotions or motivate the listeners to some sort of action. Refer to the purpose statement near the top of your outline. If that purpose was to cause a change in behavior or emotion, this type of conclusion might be the best. Some conclusions may do more than one of these things.

Miriam was given as an example of a character study earlier in this chapter. The conclusion of that lesson would vary depending on the purpose of the lesson. If the purpose was to teach women about the life of Miriam, the conclusion would remind the audience about the three cameo appearances Miriam had in the Old Testament. If the purpose was to glean lessons modern women might learn from Miriam, the conclusion might ask if the people in the audience were using their mouths to get help for others, to praise God, or to undermine the leadership God set in place as Miriam did. If the purpose was to encourage women to use their mouths for good, the conclusion might appeal to the audience to use their mouths for encouragement and praise.

Qualities of a Good Conclusion

Just like the introduction, the conclusion should be brief. Words should be chosen carefully for maximum impact. Second, it ought to be personal and relate to the listeners. They should know how the lesson is relevant in their own lives. Third, the conclusion must be specific. What was the purpose of the lesson? The conclusion reinforces that purpose. There should be no doubt as to what your desire is for the listeners. Fourth, if you are motivating listeners, the conclusion needs to be forceful and persuasive. You do not need to brow beat the audience with a guilt trip, but leave no doubt what you long for their response to be.

A positive conclusion may be more effective than a negative one. Let's take a look at Layne's conclusion to the "Courier New" chapel talk at FHU:

> You see, the load of the cross is not a light one. My dad was flipping through a religious magazine one time, and a picture caught his eye. In the picture was a group of people walking, and in the middle of the group was a man who was carrying a cross on his shoulders. The

caption of the picture explained that the people were participating in a "Walk for Christ," the purpose of which was to demonstrate that anyone who wants to follow Christ first has to take up his cross. But Dad said that as he looked at the picture, he noticed something funny about it. He wasn't sure at first, but as he looked closer, he was certain of it. There, barely visible through the legs of the crowd, he could make out wheels on the cross. The man hadn't been carrying that cross; he'd been rolling it. And so have I. As I come to Christ with the question, "What must I do to inherit eternal life," my Savior answers, "Quit looking for the easy way out, take up your cross, and come, follow Me."

As you conclude the lesson, remember that everything you have said so far has led you to this part. Therefore, do not introduce new material. You are summarizing, applying and motivating, not informing. Next, do not drag the conclusion out, wandering aimlessly in your ideas. Remember, your thoughts at this time should be brief, specific and clear.

Do not use too much humor. This is a serious time when you want to make an impact to be remembered. Finally, do not use multiple conclusions. The conclusion is reinforcing the purpose of the lesson. A lesson has a single purpose; consequently there will be a single conclusion.

Writing a Rough Draft

Now that you have an introduction, a discussion outline and a conclusion, you may want to write a rough draft of your lesson. Doing this may help you choose the most effective words and phrases to make your point. It will also help you develop correct sentence structure. However, when you present the lesson, do not read the manuscript to your audience. Following the outline will allow you to have more flexibility and speak more naturally in your delivery.

As you develop your lesson, make sure the thoughts you present are biblical and well-organized. Make sure they are relevant to your audience. Then present the lesson in your own unique style. Realize the message is more important than the messenger. The speaker is merely an instrument through which God can deliver His message to others. We are not teaching or speaking to heap glory on ourselves, but to give the glory to God (Matthew 5:16). Our motivation must be love of God, love of Christ's church, and love of mankind (1 Corinthians 13:1).

Go and teach (Matthew 28:19-20)!

Activities

1. Select one of these passages – Psalm 1:1-3; Proverbs 3:5-10; Romans 12:1-2 – and write a title and purpose statement for a lesson based on that text.

2. Select one of these Bible characters – Mary, the mother of Jesus; Daniel; Abigail – and determine the main points you might use in a lesson on that person. Arrange the points in time sequence.

3. Identify two or three types of logical order and give a contemporary example of each.

4. What are some biblical concepts that might need clarifying as you teach? How could you clarify that concept?

5. Why are the introduction and conclusion of a lesson so important?

6. Find some poems, stories, quotes, etc., that might be used to introduce a lesson. Begin a file with these items.

7. When would you want to use different types of conclusions?

8. Using the texts or characters from questions 1-5, write a conclusion and introduction to go with the points you used.

Chapter 7

Developing
A Character
Study

Cynthia Dianne Guy

Have you come out of an inspiring Bible class thinking, "What a great lesson! I wish I could teach like that"? You can. Developing an informative and interesting Bible message is not rocket science. It simply takes a love for God's Word and a little know-how for organizing ideas. This lesson will present some tools and techniques to help you create inspirational Bible lessons. The following 10 steps will guide you.

Step 1: Decide on a Biblical Subject

The first step to writing a biblical lesson is to choose a biblical subject. It may be tempting to search elsewhere for relevant ideas, but God designed Scripture to supply all our needs (2 Timothy 3:16-17). Tom Holland warns, "God forbid that one with the awesome task or responsibility of declaring God's Truth become a mere reporter of the passing scene ... that material for sermons [lessons] come from latest best-sellers, current hit movies, leading magazines, and daily newspapers." [1]

Let us not underestimate the desire for truth. Christian women are just as hungry for the Word in ladies classes as they are in the Sunday assembly; therefore, "uplifting but light" should not describe the menu for our periods of Bible study.[2]

When deciding on a subject, consider the audience's needs. A class on dating for teenage girls should include modesty and self-control. Young mothers, who seek advice on marriage and parenting, would enjoy principles from the Song of Solomon and Proverbs. Older women need to hear the Titus 2:3 directives to be holy, not slanderers, not addicted to wine, and to teach good things to younger women. These are as important as studies on angels and the Holy Spirit. We need messages that spur us to evangelism, warn us about fleshly lusts, and motivate us to emulate the faith of Sarah. A balanced diet of spiritual topics best nourishes our souls.

Sometimes the topic is pre-determined. Let's say you have volunteered to prepare a lesson for ladies class. Your topic is "Sarah," the first in a series on women of the Bible. "How do I begin?" you wonder. Let's work to develop a topical lesson on Sarah. Character studies produce rich and inspiring material on the lives of biblical role models. Also called biographical studies, these "are usually divided by either the great events or the great qualities of the character's life."[3]

To write about Sarah, you must learn about her. Go to Scripture first. It is the only inspired resource. The Genesis account introduces your subject as Sarai, half-sister and wife of Abraham. She is a woman of physical beauty, desired by kings (Genesis 12:14-15; 20:2). With her husband, she left her home to follow God's call (12:4-5). Although barren, she was promised a son (11:30; 17:19). After years of waiting, she suggested that her handmaid be used to fulfill the promise (16:1-2). The result evoked jealousy (16:4-6). When the promise was reaffirmed, she laughed (18:12). Sarah is the only woman to whom God gave a sacramental name[4] (17:15), and the only woman in Scripture whose exact age is given, whose age at death is given, and whose grave is mentioned (17:17; 23:1, 19). It is important to take copious notes, for you never know what information will be useful later.

A Bible concordance is a helpful tool. Many Bibles include a limited one in the back. *Strong's New Exhaustive Concordance of the Bible* lists all references to Sarah. Not all occur in Genesis. Hebrews 11:11 informs us that by faith she was able to conceive and bear Isaac. It names her as one of two women listed among Old Testament faithfuls. In 1 Peter 3:6, Sarah is called an example of submission for Christian women.

Zondervan's Pictorial Encyclopedia of the Bible is an excellent resource for topical studies. Under "Sarah," you find information similar to your notes. With scripture references, it identifies Sarah and summarizes the story of her move, her beauty, her plight of barrenness, her plot involving Hagar, Ishmael's birth, her jealousy, the promise of Isaac, her laughter, her faith, her motherhood, her death, and commendation as a role model. You may consult other biblical resources, such as *Nave's Topical Bible*. The idea is to have a good biblical overview of your subject before beginning the lesson.

You can gain from the study of others by perusing biblical commentaries, Christian magazines, taped or printed sermons, and good books. *The Women of the Bible* by Herbert Lockyer describes Sarah as chosen by God to become "the joint fountainhead of the great Jewish race."[5] Nick Hamilton, in his 2001 Freed-Hardeman lecture, suggests a pattern of faithfulness seen in Sarah's obedience as she followed Abraham to an unknown destination.[6] Katherine Cook, in a journal article, explains that a barren womb in Sarah's day was considered a curse, a punishment for some sin she had committed and, for some women, it nullified the major reason for their existence.[7] In his commentary on Hebrews, Charles Carter adds, "No situation gave greater cause for anxious concern in patriarchal times, as is true among primitive people to the present, than the threat of childlessness, especially a son … . It was the first son who bore the family name, inherited the family possessions, and continued the family after his father's death."[8]

You might find such enlightening resources in your church library. Brotherhood sermons and articles can be located online at www.acu.edu/rsi/index.php. This website is for the Restoration Serials Index (RSI). Under "search," change the keyword to "subject" and type in "Sarah." Twenty-eight citations are given for "Sarah (Bible Character)." Contact the publisher or a Christian university library for copies of the article. It is worth the effort. Reading widely enriches our understanding of the subject, and provides numerous ideas for the lesson's main points, sub-points and supporting material.

When you have a good understanding of your subject, it's time to put your ideas on paper. One brainstorming technique is called mind-mapping or the bubble method. Take a large sheet of paper. Write the subject in the middle and draw a circle around the words. Draw 10 lines extending out from the circle, like rays on a sun. Then, let your imagination flow. Write on each line an idea relating to your subject. You might write (1) wife of Abraham, (2) lied about their relationship, (3) barren, (4) suggested Abraham "go in unto" Hagar, (5) jealous over Ishmael's birth, (6) laughed at God's promise, (7) conceived after menopause, (8) named among the faithful, (9) followed Abraham to Canaan, (10) died at age 127. This technique produces more ideas than you will use in one lesson.

Step 2: Select the Aspect of the Subject to Be Presented

Sarah is a very broad subject. You cannot adequately cover every aspect of her life in one class period. A good lesson should emphasize one major facet of the subject. Donald Miller explains it this way: The lesson "should be a bullet, not bird shot. It ought to be designed to hit the hearer in one vital spot, rather than to spray him with scattered theological ideas unrelated to each other which touch him mildly in a dozen places." [9] What do you want your listeners to take away from this lesson?

The bubble exercise offers possible focal points: Sarah's example as a wife, her role in God's plan, her doubts shown in Hagar's conception, her laughter at the promise, her human imperfections – impatience and jealousy, her motherhood, and her faith. You think, "Her example of faith is certainly something we should emulate, but, isn't Sarah most remembered for her scheme concerning Hagar and her laughter at God's promise?" Donald Guthrie, in his Hebrews commentary, voices the apparent conflict, "It is perhaps surprising to find Sarah spoken of as an example of faith, for according to Genesis she was more conspicuous as an example of doubt." [10] A lesson about Sarah's faith must address her two reactions of "doubt."

Step 3: Select an Appropriate Scripture

You need to find a scripture that confirms Sarah's faith. As you browse your notes, Hebrews 11:11 stands out: "Through faith also Sarah herself received strength to conceive seed, and was delivered of a child when she was past age, because she judged him faithful who had promised" (KJV). This verse verifies a faith so great that she was able to have a child in her old age and to be listed with other great examples. From these truths, you can create your purpose sentence and main points.

Step 4: Write a Theme/Purpose Statement

A theme or purpose statement is foundational to a topical lesson. It gives direction by stating the main spiritual thought to be discussed. Your purpose is to present Sarah as a role model of faith. Charles L. Brown offers helpful insights in his 2001 East Tennessee School of Preaching Lecture, "Sarah, An Example for Modern Women." He observes that she "left an example by rising above her sins and failures in life. Though a tremendous example of womanhood, Sarah was completely human." [11] That is what you want your listeners to grasp in this lesson. From this, you can mold a purpose statement: "Sarah is an example of faith because she rose above her sins and failures, and, in the end, was commended by God." Your outline is shaping up nicely.

Subject: Sarah

Topic: Sarah's faith

Text: "Through faith also Sarah herself received strength to conceive seed, and was delivered of a child when she was past age, because she judged him faithful who had promised" (Hebrews 11:11 KJV).

Purpose statement: The student will see Sarah as an example of faith because she rose above her sins.

The theme is the single most important part of the lesson because it is "precisely and only" what you want your audience to take away. [12] From this point forward, all the other parts of the lesson – "main points, introduction, conclusion, supporting material – are designed to make the subject sentence hit the target." [13]

Step 5: Develop Three or Four Main Points

Now is the time to create main points that will effectively explain or support the purpose statement. James Braga suggests,

> [T]o insure that the message will be thoroughly biblical in content, we must start with a biblical subject or topic. The main divisions … must be drawn from this biblical topic, and each main division must be supported by a Scripture reference. The verses which support the main divisions should usually be drawn from portions of the Bible which are more or less widely separated from one another. [14]

Braga suggests using any one of five interrogative adverbs to connect the theme to the main points: why, how, what, when or where. [15] You will develop main points by asking, "What major actions in Sarah's life seem to concern her faith? From your bubble exercise, you find two that speak positively: her faithfulness as a wife and her motherhood in old age, and two that seem to speak negatively: her suggestion that Abraham "go in unto"

Hagar and her laughter at God's promise. These four will serve as your main points. Here is your basic outline.

Sarah demonstrated faithfulness as a wife.

Sarah persuaded Abraham to "go in unto" Hagar.

Sarah laughed at the declaration that she would bear the child.

Sarah had faith to conceive and bear Isaac.

As noted, not all of your ideas can serve as main points. Some will make good sub-points. Others may not fit the theme at all.

Step 6: Find Appropriate Verses for Points and Sub-points

The topic and main points form the skeleton of a lesson. You must now put meat on the bones. This enrichment process includes selecting a specific text to support each main point, and then adding sub-points.

Review your list of scriptures on Sarah to find one that best supports the first main point – her faithfulness as a wife. First Peter 3:6 is a good choice: "Sarah obeyed Abraham, calling him lord." Then, select appropriate texts for the others.

I. Sarah demonstrated faithfulness as a wife (1 Peter 3:6).

II. Sarah persuaded her husband to "go in to" Hagar (Genesis 16:2).

III. Sarah laughed at the declaration that she would bear the child (Genesis 18:12).

IV. Sarah had faith to conceive and bear the child of promise (Hebrews 11:11).

Next, sub-points must be developed under each main point. Take a new sheet of paper and write "faithfulness as a wife" in the center. Circle it, and draw 10 lines extending from it. Brainstorm ideas answering an interrogative question, like "How did Sarah demonstrate faithfulness as a wife?"

Suggestions include: Sarah left Ur with Abraham; she followed him to an unknown destination; she lied twice to protect him; she helped feed strangers; she obeyed him; she called him lord; and she is commended as an example. From these, choose a few sub-points to support the first main point. Follow the same procedure to create sub-points for the other main points. Your outline is one to be proud of.

I. Sarah demonstrated faithfulness as a wife (1 Peter 3:6).
   A. She followed Abraham to an unknown destination (Genesis 12:1-5).
   B. She lied to protect him in Egypt and Gerar (Genesis 12:10-20; 20:1-17).
   C. She is commended as an example for Christian wives today (1 Peter 3:6).

II. Sarah persuaded her husband to "go in to" Hagar (Genesis 16:2).
   A. Sarah was barren; yet, God promised Abraham descendants (Genesis 12:2).
   B. Sarah waited patiently many years.
   C. She believed God had restrained her from bearing (Genesis 16:2).
   D. Custom dictated arranging for a surrogate. Examples: Rachel and Leah (Genesis 30). [16]

III. Sarah laughed at the declaration that she would bear the child (Genesis 18:12).
   A. She was 90 years old (Genesis 17:17).
   B. She had passed menopause (Genesis 18:11).
   C. The Lord gently rebuked, "Is anything too hard for the Lord?" (Genesis 18:14).
   D. "Her unbelief was overcome, and she ultimately credited the Divine Promise." [17]

IV. Sarah had faith to conceive and bear the child of promise (Hebrews 11:11).
   A. She needed power beyond herself (Genesis 18:11).
   B. She heard the words herself and believed (Genesis 18:10-15; Hebrews 11:11).
   C. Her faith is commended (Hebrews 11:11).

Much time and effort have been invested in the outline. More preparation is necessary for an excellent lesson. North warns, "Nothing is more disconcerting to a listener than to sit for thirty minutes and hear 4,500 words thrown at him with nothing in any apparent order." [18] Earnest instructors should never be guilty of insufficient research or ineffective organization; they realize that haphazard presentations embarrass any self-respecting teacher. [19]

Step 7: Create a Hook – an Interesting Introduction

With the most difficult work finished, you are ready to write. Like all lessons, yours must have a beginning. This is called the introduction. It may be from a sentence to a short paragraph in length. A lively or interesting beginning, called a hook, works well to grab the attention of listeners. Blackwood suggests, "Use a contemporary approach in presenting a biblical truth. This way of starting calls for emphasis on the topic." [20] Quotations, questions and anecdotes make great hooks.

The introduction tells listeners what the lesson is about. Some writers create it after they finish the lesson. Their reason is the same as those who wait to title a book or movie. They are, then, "better able to think of an introduction which is suited to the message." [21] Many write the introduction first.

In this case, use an attention-grabbing anecdote as a hook, followed by the introduction:

> The article "All Kneecaps Look Alike" in the May 2000 *Christian Woman* magazine featured a little girl coming out of Bible class with a picture of Sarah holding baby Isaac. A woman asked her, "Is that a picture of Sarah?" A serious look came over the face of the youngster, who said solemnly, "Sarah had a baby when she was old." She paused a second and said, "Really old!" After another pause she plucked up the skin on the back of her hand with her thumb and forefinger and with a grimace, added, "Bumpy old!" [22]

Our lesson today is about this wonderful Old Testament role model and example of faith. Most of us heard the familiar stories of Sarah when we were little girls. We learned about her faithfulness as Abraham's wife, her scheme for using Hagar to fulfill God's promise, her laughter at the promise, and her miraculous motherhood when she was "bumpy old."

This last sentence of the introduction will transition smoothly into the first sentence of the main body: "First, let's talk about her example as a faithful wife to Abraham."

Step 8: Gather Meaningful Illustrations

This step is the fun part – putting flesh on the skeleton and making the lesson come alive! Our outline provides a spiritually rich and organized pattern, but you cannot simply read it to the class. The points need meaningful illustrations to give them more force, more appeal and more vigor. [23] To enrich the first subpoint, that Sarah followed Abraham to an unknown destination, you might quote Lottie Beth Hobbs in *Daughters of Eve*, "Together with her husband, Sarah accepted this unprecedented challenge to take a new step of faith and follow God into the unknown. She also had to leave friends and loved ones and familiar surroundings to face the perils and anxieties of an uncertain future." [24] This quote truly propels the message of Sarah's faithfulness.

You want your listeners to feel Sarah's frustration with her inability to conceive. Personal experiences connect well with audiences. If you have dealt with infertility, you might briefly mention your own devastating experience. The earlier quotes from Cook and Carter fit well here, along with John H. Walton's, in his commentary on Genesis. He explains the custom for childless women, "Marriage contracts from the town of Nuzi in the middle of the second millennium B.C. stipulate that if the wife turns out to be barren, she should provide the husband with a surrogate child-bearer." [25] Eugenia Price, in *God Speaks to Women Today*, concurs, "The custom dictated that if the wife could not bear a child, then she must arrange for the service of someone who could." [26] The accounts of Rachel and Leah using their handmaids to produce children (Genesis 30) would add understanding.

Focus on the fact that Sarah was human. After Abraham received the promise of a child, Sarah waited patiently for at least 10 years. Then, at age 75, "the possibility of ever becoming a mother died in her heart." [27] Cook asks us to consider Sarah's action, not one of faithlessness, but one of desperation and sacrifice:

> With what had to be an act of selflessness, she decided that the only way Abraham could become a father was through another woman. ... We who know the end of the story can easily declare her to be foolish and even callous, but how many of us would wait until it seemed impossible for our prayers to be answered without taking action ourselves? [28]

Let us not forget that Abraham, called "Father of the Faithful," willingly participated in Sarah's plan. It was he who, earlier, had asked her to lie (Genesis 12:10-20) and in 17:17, Abraham also laughed at the promise of a child in their old age. "One of the beautiful things about the Bible," notes Bobbie Jobe in her book, *Sarah's Story*, "is that we are told both the good points and bad points about each character." [29]

Did Sarah's laughter disqualify her as a subject of faith? Bruce K. Waltke, in his Genesis commentary states, "Her body was procreatively dead." [30] Was laughter not a human reaction? Gordon J. Wenham, in his commentary proposes,

> She laughed not out of cocky arrogance, but because a life of long disappointment had taught her not to clutch at straws. Hopelessness, not pride, underlay her unbelief. Her self-restraint in not openly expressing her doubts and the sadness behind them go far to explain the gentleness of the divine rebuke. [31]

When the Lord rebuked Sarah, she kept silent. Her silence was "an evidence of her conviction; her subsequent conception was a proof of her repentance and forgiveness." [32]

Meaningful illustrations beef up a lesson. Resources are rich and varied. Stafford North states that "the Bible itself should be the primary source of supporting material." [33] He also suggests using quotes from commentaries, theological works, poetical literature, hymns, historical works and encyclopedias. Factual information may include factual data (such as the Nuzi law), figures, statistics, historical data, dates, geographical information, archaeological findings, scientific discoveries or even current events. [34] Narratives, real or hypothetical events in the life of a person or group, are also valuable. [35]

Remember to give credit to the real authors of any material used in your lesson. Also, closely follow your outline. There is often a temptation to secularize – getting too far away from the biblical issue and turning the class into a forum for hot topics. For example, while talking about Sarah's scheme concerning Hagar, you might trail off into discussions of surrogate motherhood and in vitro fertilization. Mentioning them is fine, but Blackwood warns against topical lessons that are wholly secular, "Since the lay hearers come out of a world where they must listen to the cash register and share in the rush of the market place, why should they not in church hear something other than the lingo of the street?" [36]

Step 9: Give an Appropriate Application

Your interesting and informative main body is nearly complete. Your lesson needs an application that supports the theme that Sarah is an example of faith. Neale Pryor, in a 1991 Harding University lecture, noted, "Often the greatest test of our faith is waiting. The silence of God is sometimes the hardest part of life to deal with. It is hard to realize that God does not run on the same schedule that humans do." [37] Sarah failed at times. She "was a woman of the flesh just like you, with both weaknesses and strengths." [38] She rose above her sins and failures in life and inspires us to do the same. [39] Guilt and despair should not overwhelm us. We should draw hope and courage from Sarah's story, for God keeps His promises.

Step 10: End With a Dynamic Conclusion

The conclusion sums up the lesson. Louis Rushmore states,

> [U]se the Introduction to tell your listeners what you're going to tell them, in the Body tell them what you have to tell them, and in the Conclusion tell your auditors what you've told them. This procedure makes use of the time honored, crowd-tested tool of repetition. Of course, both the Introduction and the Conclusion are abbreviated versions of information contained in the Body. [40]

A conclusion for your lesson about Sarah might go something like this:

> I pray that this lesson has helped us to see Sarah as an example of faith. She demonstrated great faithfulness as a wife and patiently waited – longer than many of us would have – before succumbing to the temptation to "help God out." But when she was old – yes, "bumpy old" – "Through faith also Sara herself received strength to conceive seed, and was delivered of a child when she was past age because she judged him faithful who had promised."

The last sentence should stand out. Freelance writer Eva Shaw suggests, "If you're still floundering for the perfect punch line, or ending sentence, review your hook and rewrite it for the end. Whatever you do with the end, make it quick. Do it in one short paragraph." [41]

After writing a lesson, it is helpful to set it aside for a day or two, and then reread it. It may take several edits before you are satisfied. In the end you may realize that although you didn't know you could write, it really doesn't involve rocket science – just a love for God's Word and a little know-how for organizing ideas.

Activities

1. Choose three biblical subjects in which you are interested. Choose one from a favorite verse, another from a psalm or proverb, and the third, a character from a Bible story. Do the following exercises for each.

2. Use a concordance to look up scriptures that include your subject. You may find *Zondervan's Pictorial Encyclopedia* or a topical Bible helpful for subjects with numerous scripture references. Get a good biblical overview of the subject.

3. Find two good Bible commentaries and examine comments on key verses. For example, the *Pulpit Commentary* presents enlightening facts concerning first-century widows in its volume containing 1 Timothy 5.

4. Read about your subject. Find good books. Browse your church library or a Christian university library, or seek out church members with good religious books. Also, find good articles. Go online as instructed in this chapter to find the "Restoration Serials Index." Enter the subject or scripture in the "keyword" box (or drop down to Subject). Limit broad subjects by entering a second subject. For instance, "love" yields 1697 brotherhood articles; but entering "Christian" in the second box yields 71 articles specifically on Christian love. Entering "children" in the second box yields 13 articles on loving our children.

5. Brainstorm using the bubble method. Write your subject in the middle of a large sheet of paper and jot down 10 aspects of it. Let your imagination flow. Select one aspect of the subject on which to focus. For example: Christian love.

6. Select an appropriate text. For example: John 13:35.

7. Write a phrase or sentence stating the main spiritual thought to be discussed. For example: People will know we are Christians by our love.

8. Develop three or four main points by using an interrogative adverb: why, how, what, when or where. For example, "What are some ways we show Christian love?" The main points could be:

> I. Loving our family
> II. Loving our neighbors
> III. Loving our enemies
> IV. Loving God

9. Find appropriate verses for the main points.

10. Develop three or four sub-points under main points. Use the bubble method. For example: "How do we show love to our family?" The sub-points could be:

> I. Loving our family, Titus 2:4
>   A. Loving our husbands, Titus 2:4; Proverbs 31:11-12
>   B. Loving our children, Titus 2:4; Proverbs 22:6; Ephesians 6:4
>   C. Loving our parents, Matthew 15:4; Ephesians 6:2; 1 Timothy 5:4

11. Create a hook from an interesting quotation, poem, question or anecdote.

12. Gather meaningful illustrations.

13. Give an appropriate application for readers to take away and apply.

14. Create a dynamic conclusion by summing up the lesson and, perhaps, revisiting your hook.

Chapter 8

Public
Speaking

Amanda Box

S peaking is literally one of my favorite things to do. Of course, I'm not exactly normal. I chose to go into the communication field and always knew exactly what I wanted to do. I pursued a master's degree in communication and continued in a career of teaching and consulting. Most normal people don't like public speaking – not only don't like it, but also avoid it like the plague. I understand; I'm the weird one. But I also understand that God gave you a message that only you can deliver and that public speaking isn't as hard as you think.

I also understand that you will be nervous. This is actually a good sign. It simply means you want to do a good job. My nervousness usually starts after I agree to speak. I feel intense pressure when women give up a Saturday morning or even a weekend to be at an event where I'm speaking. I completely understand that women have to work really hard to arrange to be away from home on a weekend. Even on Wednesday night, I know that getting to Bible class is sometimes a difficult task. My prayer is that God puts words in my mouth and a spirit of searching in my heart to say the right thing to the right person. And although the emphasis of the class or ladies day is not my performance, I desire to teach God's Word in a motivating and inspiring way. I never want someone to leave after one of my classes wishing she had stayed home.

Start Out Small: Read Scripture Aloud

One way to get used to speaking in front of a group of people is to volunteer to read scripture aloud at an event or class. To overcome your nervousness or fear of reading in front of a group of women, be well prepared. Go over the scripture that you have been assigned. Make sure that you comprehend all the words included in the text and that you can pronounce proper names. You may need to consult a Bible dictionary or a self-pronouncing Bible for help.

Read the text aloud in private. Practice projecting to your audience rather than bending your head over your Bible. If you have trouble reading from your small print Bible, copy the text from Bible software. You can enlarge the text to any font needed. Highlight your text so that the reading becomes more visible.

As you approach the podium or lectern on the day of the event, announce clearly and distinctly the passage to be read. Repeat, if necessary and look at your audience. This will help clear any butterflies that remain. Read at a comfortable pace, taking breaths at periods or commas. Read with confidence and conviction – after all, you are delivering God's Word to your audience.

Just as reading Scripture aloud takes practice, so does moving to the next step of speaking before an audience.

Make a Plan

One of the first things that I want you to understand is that public speaking is a process, and it takes organization and planning. This chapter will take you step by step toward making your own plan. Great speakers don't just open their mouths and become eloquent. It takes as much work as it does talent. You may not feel like you are a great speaker, but by the time you have finished making your plan, you will be in great shape to practice a few times and then speak in front of others. So read on and begin making a plan. Read the whole chapter first and then get started on your presentation.

Step 1: What Is Your Passion?

Choosing a topic can be a difficult thing to do. Some mistakenly think that the topic itself is either boring or exciting. Not true. The reality is that the speaker will determine whether a topic is effective or not. Be sure to consider your audience. How old are they? Where are they spiritually? What is the occasion? How much time do you have? Every variable surrounding the occasion will determine the specifics of your topic.

A really important consideration is to ask yourself what you are passionate about. As women, we have a special talent for reaching an emotional level of spirituality that creates an intense bond between believers. What in your spiritual life or biblical study makes you feel intense emotion: happiness, fear, comfort, amazement, anger? If you feel intense emotion about a topic, then it will naturally come out in your voice, provided you have a good plan. As a unique individual, you have something to offer the audience that no one else can. So take what you are passionate about and combine that with what you know. Think about experiences, interests, hobbies, skills or people that you know a lot about. Those two things are a great combination because when you take a spiritual subject about which you feel intense passion and combine that with a familiar topic, you have a winning combination. Never worry about if your topic is good enough or exciting enough. If you have the combination of passion and knowledge, then you are ready to go. The most effective speakers speak from the heart about personal subjects.

Let's say you feel passionate about evangelism and have been on a mission trip. After you have chosen a topic, decide what the purpose of your speech is. Do you want to inform or persuade or entertain?

If you want to persuade others to be more evangelistic, write a purpose statement: "The audience will be persuaded to be more evangelistic." Do not leave out this step. It will determine every other part of the speaking influence. You must set a goal.

Now that you have a purpose statement, write a central idea. Boil your speech down to one sentence. What is the main idea you want to communicate?

Central idea: "Jesus commanded all Christians to go into the entire world and preach." The central idea will keep you focused. All speech content must fit under this main idea.

However, if nothing comes to mind, there are several other ways to choose a topic:

1. Choose a Bible character and do a character study.

2. Take a passage of Scripture and develop a presentation.

3. Consider how to group topics under broad headings. Here are some examples:

• Places – where Jesus taught; churches that received letters from Paul;

• Events – angelic visitations; Satanic appearances;

• Processes – those Jesus raised from the dead; God's use of nature;

• Concepts – the Christian graces; the fruit of the Spirit;

• Problems – how to forgive; how to overcome temptation.

Develop other potential topics under these headings.

4. Go through the alphabet and write down what comes to mind for A, B, C, etc. Don't worry about quality, just make a list, and when you get to Z, go back and evaluate for good topics.

Step 2: Research

Now that you have selected your topic and you know what you want to accomplish, what next? Gather information. Allowing enough time for research is crucial. You want to have time to study and to think about how all the pieces fit together. You also need time to gather effective stories and illustrations that will interest the audience and perhaps get them emotionally involved.

Having outside sources in addition to your Bible will help you look at your topic from another's perspective, and it will add to your credibility. I suggest at least three. By studying other sources, you will find quotes, stories, illustrations and information that will be great additions to your presentation. Chapters six and seven discuss these topics in more depth.

As you go through your information, take notes on everything you want to include in your speech. It's a good idea to use note cards for each piece of information along with the page number and scripture or source. After you think you have enough information, put the cards in a logical order. Once you get the body of your speech in a rough order, you can then turn your attention to the introduction and conclusion.

Step 3: Introduction and Conclusion

By far the most important part of your speech is your introduction. The introduction must have high emotional content, and it must be polished. An effective introduction will immediately grab the listeners' attention and draw them into your speech. It doesn't matter how helpful, truthful or brilliant your content is – people will not be listening to you unless you have a strong introduction.

Follow the pattern of Jesus and use stories to bring the audience in. Your own personal story is generally the best because you can tell it with ease and emotion without too much practice. People love to feel a wide range of emotions including excitement, fear and humor. Shocking or surprising statistics are a good way to grab attention. Great quotes or scripture work really well in an introduction, too, capturing an idea in a creative way. Poetry can also be effective if it isn't too long.

A short list of "don'ts" of introductions might be helpful. Including items from the don't list in your introduction will communicate to your audience that you didn't prepare very well and that there is nothing worthwhile to look forward to.

• Don't say, "Today I'm going to talk about ..."

• Don't ask a cliché rhetorical question such as, "How many of you have ever said something you regret?"

• Don't apologize for your abilities. If you tell the audience you are a sorry speaker, then they will believe it, no matter what kind of job you do. Your job is to look confident on the outside no matter how you feel on the inside.

The conclusion uses basically the same principles as the introduction. The purpose of the conclusion is to heighten the impact of your speech. Be sure it has a high emotional content to illustrate the factual content from the body of your speech.

Most importantly, end on time. If you go over your time limit, you will be talking but no one will be listening.

Step 4: Preparation and Speaking Outlines

You should prepare two outlines before you give a speech. The first one is called a preparation outline. This is a full sentence outline including your introduction/conclusion, transitions, all of your information, and references. Usually for every 5 minutes you speak, you should have two pages of full sentence outline, single-spaced.

Do not take this outline to the podium, it is strictly for thorough organization. Another important part of the outline is to have it ready about a week before you speak. Do not start putting the outline together the night before you speak. You are setting yourself up for failure. The only thing you want to do the night before is pick out your clothes and practice a few times.

You will be tempted to skip this step because it's the most tedious part of preparing the speech. However, if you do skip it, the quality of your presentation will suffer. Creating a full sentence outline allows you to think through each main point thoroughly. The good news is that after you finish making a full sentence preparation outline, the hard part is over.

The second outline you will make is your speaking outline. Basically your speaking outline consists of prompts to remind you what to say but is much abbreviated. It could be a word outline or some combination of several things including personal notes to yourself to relax, smile or slow down. The important thing about the speaking outline is that it helps remind you what to say without being a manuscript. It should be easy to read at a glance. For most speakers a word outline with a few personal reminders works best.

Step 5: Delivery Style

The most effective style is called extemporaneous speaking style. It is a cross between impromptu (completely spontaneous) and memorization. There is no need to memorize your whole speech. It's too hard and isn't effective. But you do want to practice so that you are polished without being stiff. The goal is to sound conversational and professional. Your speaking outline will prompt you about what to say, so that you can talk intelligently about what you have studied. Reading your speech is not allowed – ever. As you speak conversationally, remember to use correct grammar.

Step 6: Nonverbal/Body Language

Projecting confidence in your nonverbal communication is essential. As you walk to the podium, walk slowly with your head up. Don't make any derogatory comments to friends on your way. It will only hurt your credibility. You may be shaking on the inside, but how you look on the outside is what is important. Smile.

When you are ready for the first words of your introduction, be sure to take your time, look up, then talk. This is a small thing with very big consequences. Look – then talk. Don't rush. Chances are your nerves will cause you to speak a little faster and softer in the beginning, and this plan will help you calm down and sound confident.

Confident body language will determine the effectiveness of your speech. Any kind of nervousness usually comes out through something physical such as rocking, leaning, fidgeting with hair or hands, saying "um" and "okay." So, if you are aware of what you do when you are nervous, you can make a plan. If you know you tend to play with your hair, plan to hold your notes with both hands or place your hands on the lip of the podium. Have a home base for your hands when they aren't completing a task.

Stand with your feet shoulder width apart to avoid any rocking or leaning. Be sure to stand up straight and avoid leaning on the podium. Always keep in mind that you want to send a confident message to your audience. Again, you may not feel confident, but you can still look confident. It is perfectly acceptable to fake it.

Be sure to speak with enthusiasm and direct eye contact. It is all right to look down to check your notes. Just make sure you are looking at the audience far more than you are looking down.

I have a great solution for you if you are worried about saying "ands" and "ums." First, you must understand that your brain likes to play tricks on you. The time in your head is kind of like slow motion, and when you are speaking, your brain exaggerates any tiny bits of silence, which is why people tend to use a lot of "ums," "ands" and "okays." It feels like a long time of silence, but it really isn't to the audience. To the audience, it just feels like a normal pause, which is far better than a bunch of "ums." So understanding this, you are now ready for the magic formula. When you hear yourself saying "um," just close your mouth. It's impossible to say a bunch of "ums," "ands" and "okays" with your mouth closed. After you shut your mouth, look down, find your spot, look up and begin talking again. It really is that simple.

Dress professionally any time you are in front of an audience. Your clothes will send a very strong message. Think about your audience and occasion. Choose carefully.

Step 7: Visual Aids

There are many options for visual aids that genuinely work very well. Tangible things that an audience can see help people remember the information as well as enjoy the presentation. Visual aids can include almost anything. Many speakers use Microsoft PowerPoint, which generally provides a polished and professional look. With PowerPoint, be sure that the text is easily readable. The PowerPoint presentation should augment your speech, not replace it. Put yourself in the place of the audience and judge whether the pictures are of good quality and if any of the little bells and whistles are distracting rather than helpful.

When considering any visual aid, think about the logistics, time and equipment needed. Is it big enough for everyone to see? Try to avoid poster board, passing objects or anything distracting.

Step 8: Practice

If you did your full sentence outline and did all the necessary planning, practice will actually be quite easy. Just work on your speaking outline as you work through the speech out loud. Be sure to time yourself. Watch yourself in a mirror or videotape yourself. Critique any nervous nonverbal fidgeting. When you get to a rough spot, stop and work out any problems. Then go back to the introduction and continue until you get stuck again. Work out the problem and then go back to the beginning and see how far you can get. After you can get through the whole speech without stopping, practice it about three more times. When you can do this, you are ready! Congratulations. The day of your speech, go somewhere by yourself and run through it one or two more times.

Now you are ready to go. My best advice is to prepare and relax. Be sure to use positive visualization. Mentally picture yourself delivering your speech successfully and then go through all the steps to prepare. Do your very best at studying God's Word and organizing properly. Practice adequately. On the day of your speech relax your body as much as possible. Breathe slowly, relax any tensed muscles. If you follow the steps mentioned in this chapter, you will have a quality presentation.

Activities

1. Begin making a list of possible topics for future speeches by using the alphabet suggestion mentioned earlier in this chapter. Write down what comes to mind for A, B, C, etc. Don't worry about quality, just make a list, and when you get to Z, go back and evaluate for good topics.

2. Make your own list of topics as mentioned earlier in this chapter. List a few things in each of these categories – places, events, processes, concepts, problems. This will give you a list of topics to choose from.

3. What would be some reliable sources for statistics on divorce, sexually transmitted disease, women working outside the home, etc.?

Chapter 9

Leading
Prayer

Debbie Bumbalough

As a child our first prayers usually revolved around meal times or bedtime. We were taught a pattern to follow and added embellishments as we grew more confident in praying aloud. Those early prayers, although heartfelt, usually reflected the limits of our mental and spiritual growth. As each of us grow older and gain strength in our spiritual training, our prayers should also be a reflection of that spiritual growth.

When Paul admonished the Colossians to "[c]ontinue earnestly in prayer, being vigilant in it with thanksgiving" (4:2), his letter was meant for both men and women of the "saints and faithful brethren" (1:2). Women pray along with the men in the public assembly of the church. However, as Paul instructed Timothy in 1 Timothy 2:11-12, as women we are exhorted to submit to men. Women can *pray* at any time; women cannot *lead* prayer in public worship when men are present.

Because women desire the fellowship of other women, they sometimes find themselves in the position of being called on to lead prayer in a ladies class, at a ladies day or retreat, or other situations where only women are present. Because prayer is a vital part of our public and private worship, women should be prepared to lead other women. Although our early training in prayer may have been heartfelt, our public prayers should have more format and purpose. This chapter will endeavor to help women to overcome the fear of leading women in public prayer and provide help in developing prayers that will encompass the needs of various audiences.

Prayer – An Important Part of Our Daily Lives

Thayer's *Lexicon* defines prayer as a petition for one's self or an intercession for others. Mankind has an inner need to pray and worship. The writer of Psalm 42 declares, "As the deer pants for the water brooks, So pants my soul for You, O God. My soul thirsts for God, for the living God" (vv. 1-2). Abraham Lincoln has been quoted as saying, "I have been driven many times to my knees by the overwhelming conviction that I had nowhere else to go. My own wisdom and that of all about me seemed insufficient for that day." [1]

The author of Hebrews tells us, "But without faith it is impossible to please Him, for he who comes to God must believe that He is, and that He is a rewarder of those who diligently seek Him." We must seek God through prayer for praise and thanksgiving of God's goodness and mercy. Confessing the name of Jesus before His Father and admitting our faults are two important aspects of our prayers.

We are assured that when we bring requests before God our prayers will be answered. "Let us therefore come boldly to the throne of grace, that we may obtain mercy and find grace to help in time of need" (Hebrews 4:16). He alone will supply our every need, but we have to submit our requests before Him, becoming more of a worshiper through prayer than merely a presenter of a shopping list.

Prayers in the Old Testament were an important part of Hebrew history. In the patriarchal period, "men began to call on the name of the Lord" (Genesis 4:26). Prayer was associated with sacrificial worship in hopes that the offering would be fully accepted. Prayer for Abram and Jacob was on a more personal level with God. Later, the Levitical priests interceded for the Israelite nation. The priests more or less decided what prayers were to be offered for the Israelites.

Later under captivity the trials of bondage caused God's people to reflect and develop a more personal prayer life. This is evident in the habits of Daniel who went to his window at least three times every day to pray. The Psalms are an expression of sin and heartfelt contrition. J.C. Lambert in the *International Standard Bible Encyclopedia* states, "We see the loftiest flights attained by the spirit of prayer – the intense craving for pardon, purity and other spiritual blessings (Psalm 51; Psalm 130) and the most heartfelt longing for a living communion with God Himself (Psalm 63:1; Psalm 84:2)."[2]

Clearly, prayer is an important part of our daily lives. Throughout the New Testament we see how Jesus took prayer to a more personal and intimate level. We see Him in the act of prayer, and He gives us an example to serve as a model prayer. Matthew 6:9-13 is quoted, memorized and prayed by Christians everywhere.

Ancil Jenkins in his book *Lord, Teach Us to Pray* states, "No one understood and practiced prayer as Jesus did." The place of prayer in His life is well illustrated in the gospel of Luke, often called "The Gospel of Prayer."[3] Clearly, prayer was a priority in Jesus' life and should be in ours. To lead other women in prayer, we must first develop a dedicated prayer life of our own.

How to Develop a Prayer Life

Our prayers should begin with an attitude of submission. If we are submissive, our attitude will reflect the humility that God requires in order to hear our prayers. James writes, "Draw near to God and He will draw near to you" (James 4:7). And then in verse 10, "Humble yourselves in the sight of the Lord, and He will lift you up."

James, the brother of Jesus, was a praying person. The word

"prayer" is mentioned a number of times in his epistle. Historians have named him the "old camel" because his knees were callused due to frequent kneeling in prayer.[4] Early historian Hegesippus called him "a most just and righteous man." James urges us to take every need to the Lord in prayer.

> Is anyone among you suffering? Let him pray. Is anyone cheerful? Let him sing psalms. Is anyone among you sick? Let him call for the elders of the church, and let them pray over him, anointing him with oil in the name of the Lord. And the prayer of faith will save the sick, and the Lord will raise him up. And if he has committed sins, he will be forgiven. Confess your trespasses to one another, and pray for one another, that you may be healed. The effective, fervent prayer of a righteous man avails much. (James 5:13-16)

There are critical times when we find ourselves on our knees in prayer. Perhaps a phone call at 2 a.m. telling you a loved one has been taken to the hospital will cause you to drop to your knees and offer a prayer of protection for him or her. Moments like these are often spontaneous, with the petitioner feeling a need to humble herself before God before taking action. As Guy N. Woods stated in his commentary on the book of James,

> One whose desire is to learn mathematical principles would not resort to prayer but to textbooks dealing therewith; one who desires the divine wisdom must get down on his knees. Facts to be stored in the head are obtained only through mental effort; the wisdom which has its home in the depths of the soul only God can bestow.[5]

Here are some practical steps to develop a prayer life:

• Develop a pattern for your personal prayers. Discipline in prayer must be practiced because so many distractions can pull our thoughts away from the true purpose of prayer. God knows our every thought, but our prayers should be deliberate and intentional. What we offer in prayer should have more substance than merely the ramblings of our mind. Using a pattern of some kind helps us to stay on course as we pray. A widely used pattern for prayer is the acrostic "ACTS," which represents the words "adoration," "confession," "thanksgiving" and "supplication."

A Adoration – Praise God and adore Him for who He is. Acknowledge His divinity and authority over all the earth and mankind.

C Confession – Confession of sins through Christ brings us to repentance and submission. We also confess that Jesus is Lord and Master, and we ask for His forgiveness and cleansing.

T Thanksgiving – Specifically thank God for His blessings, His mercy and His care. We offer thanks for salvation through God's Son and look forward to a heavenly home.

S Supplication – Whether in our private or public prayers, we offer our wants and needs to God. We know that God will hear our requests and intercession for others. By placing supplication toward the end of our prayer, we are reminded of all the wonderful things that God has done for us. Our worries seem less anxious when praise comes first from our lips.

• Find a place and a time to pray privately. When a daily routine of prayer is established, prayer life is not only strengthened, but also anticipated. Prayer becomes a habit that you don't want to break. Jesus often went to a mountainside or a garden to pray (Matthew 14:23; 26:36). Specific prayer time is individual and personal, but it should be a priority. "Evening and morning and at noon I will pray" (Psalm 55:17).

• Pray throughout the day. Short petitions to the Father give us strength and comfort and keep us focused to "pray without ceasing" (1 Thessalonians 5:17). Many of the psalms express a cry from the heart. "O Lord my God, I cried out to You, And You healed me" (Psalm 30:2). In many psalms the phase, "Be merciful to me, O God" is used by the writer. Psalm 119:164 states, "Seven times a day I praise You, Because of Your righteous judgments."

During our daily activities we might utter similar phrases that would help us have more patience, provide strength or protection. Because Jesus intercedes our prayers offered to the heavenly Father, we have the assurance that even these petitions are heard.

• Diligent Bible study will help you format and develop your prayers. By examining the prayers of Jesus and other Bible characters, we have patterns and examples to help us acquire effective prayers. We can learn from the prayers of Old Testament characters such as Hannah (1 Samuel 2:1-10); David's prayer for his people and for his son, Solomon (1 Chronicles 29:10-19); Daniel's prayer (Daniel 9:4-19); Habakkuk's prayer of faith (Habakkuk 3:17-19); and Jonah's prayer of deliverance (Jonah 2:1-9). Many of the psalms offer praise and thanksgiving, along with David's pleas to God for redemption. In the New Testament, we read how Mary offers a prayer of praise in Luke 1:46-56. Paul prays for the churches in Ephesus, Colossae, Philippi and more throughout the epistles. The Lord's Prayer in Matthew 6:9-13 is a model given by Jesus for us to pattern.

• Keep a written prayer list for easy access. Just writing down the names of people that you want to pray for will help you remember them. Update your list daily and present the names before God for specific needs. We use our computers at work and at home to record all kinds of information, so why not our prayer lists? Also include prayers of thanksgiving for people whose illnesses have improved or for their recovery.

Leading Women in Public Prayers

Now that you have worked on developing a personal prayer life, you can begin to work on praying in public. When leading women publicly in prayer such as at a ladies day, we should remember that we are priests, much like those in the Old Testament who administered many of the prayers offered to God for the Israelite nation. We represent the entire audience when we offer our prayer to God. Peter reminds us,

But you are a chosen generation, a royal priesthood, a holy nation, His own special people, that you may proclaim the praises of Him who called you out of darkness into His marvelous light; who once were not a people but are now the people of God, who had not obtained mercy but now have obtained mercy. (1 Peter 2:9-10)

Both the Old and the New Testaments describe the people of God as "the chosen" or "elect" (Isaiah 42:1; 1 Peter 2:6). We are called to a special holiness and service to Him. Guy N. Woods states in his commentary on 1 Peter that we are also a "priesthood and we are empowered to officiate in worship [with women only] and the priesthood is a 'royal' one because of its relationship to the King." [6] Because of our unique relationship with Jesus, we should consider it a privilege to offer a prayer for other women.

Components of Public Prayer

1. To lead a public prayer a woman must first be a child of God. "If you abide in Me, and My words abide in you, you will ask what you desire, and it shall be done for you" (John 15:7). James 5:16 says that the "prayer of a righteous man [woman] is powerful and effective" (NIV).

2. As New Testament Christians we address our prayers to God through the intercession of Jesus, His Son. "For through Him we both h ve access by one Spirit to the Father" (Ephesians 2:18). Jesus instructed the disciples in John 16:23-24 to address prayer to the Father in the name of the Son. "If you ask anything in My name, I will do it" (John 14:14).

3. Public prayers should be genuine and in a language that everyone in your audience can understand. Jesus admonished us in Matthew 6:5-8 to avoid showiness and vain repetitions. Mimicking phrases from others' prayers that have been handed down throughout generations may sound familiar but still have little understanding for the average audience. Can you

imagine closing a devotional of young women and saying, "Guard, guide and direct us"? Another phrase from my childhood is, "Forgive us of our sins of omission and co-mission." It took me years to figure that one out. Vain repetitions are empty, superficial phrases that have no place in public prayers. Our prayers should avoid extravagant or flowery language.

4. Prayers should he heard. Speak with confidence and boldness (Hebrews 4:16). Articulate distinctly; hold your head up with your shoulders back. Speak loudly enough that the woman sitting on the back row can hear. Women should offer prayers confidently, believing that God will hear and answer them.

5. Be sensitive to the needs of your audience. For instance, if you know that a young mother who has recently miscarried is present, you might not want to include extensive praise for all the babies in a congregation.

6. Be prepared. Work out your formula for prayer and practice it daily. If you prefer, write out your prayer before you are to give it publicly. However, it is best if you only use a brief outline and a list of names to be prayed for. After you have become proficient at public prayer, discard your outlines and notes as they will soon become a crutch and interfere with your heartfelt worship.

7. Close your prayer in the name of Jesus. Jesus states in John 16:23-24, "And in that day you will ask Me nothing. Most assuredly, I say to you, whatever you ask the Father in My name He will give you. Until now you have asked nothing in My name. Ask, and you will receive, that your joy may be full."

Remember you are talking to God. Talk to Him and let your words come naturally. Put aside worries about what others may think or say about you. You are a priest, an ambassador of Christ, and you have the privilege of speaking to the Master for other women.

Activities

1. Write out short but heartfelt prayers that you may have uttered in a moment of distress or fear. Share them with the

class and tell how this immediate communication with God helped you in a particular situation.

2. Memorize phrases from Scripture that can actually be a part of your prayer. Write down examples found in Psalms 8:1; 9:1-2; 1 Thessalonians 5:18; and Philippians 4:6-7.

3. List some phrases that are often repeated in prayers but have meanings that are not easily understood.

4. Using the acrostic ACTS, look up scriptures using a concordance or topical index that pertains to each letter of the formula. After the verses have been collected, assemble them in a prayer. Connect the prayer with phrases to make it flow smoothly. Add a beginning address to God and close the prayer in the name of Jesus. Share your prayer with the class.

5. Why is it important to take time to pray?

6. What does Bible study add to a person's prayer life?

Chapter 10

Leading Singing

Joyce Bloomingburg

Each aspect of worship is important to strengthen our faith and encourage us. Prayer is our way to communicate to God our praise and adoration as well as our desires and wishes for His guidance and care. Bible study, whether in a class setting or in the general worship assembly, allows God to communicate to us His desire for our salvation and our walk in the Christian life. The Lord's Supper, for some, is the most important aspect of worship because we commune with God in this memorial feast only once a week, which might appear to make it more special.

For me, singing is also a special time of worship. As women we are taught to follow the lead of the men as we worship together in praise to God. In every aspect of the general worship, we listen as able men direct our thoughts in prayer or Bible study, but in the song service we are encouraged to take an active part. Singing and making melody in our hearts gives us so many ways to express our love, admiration and respect to our Lord and Savior.

When women gather for a retreat, a Bible study or a ladies day, praising God in song is usually at the top of the list. Hearing women sing together with sopranos and altos blending in sweet harmony is truly one of God's blessings. In order for all of us to worship God in unity, it is easier to sing together and in the right key if a leader is present. This is one of the areas where so many women feel that they fall short in taking a lead. I hope this chapter will better equip women who wish to take part in directing singing among women.

Because most women do not have time to study a complete music education course, here is a quick version to help you get started leading singing before the next ladies day.

First of all, most of us have sung the songs featured in today's songbooks. We know the tunes and most of the words. A quick way to learn to lead a song is to hum a few bars of the first verse. It's that easy. Sing the song through and concentrate on getting the first note somewhere in the middle range so that most women can participate. If you end up being a half of a pitch low or a half of a pitch high, it's okay. Everyone will join in and sing right along with you. You can adjust the pitch on the next verse.

Second, practice singing the song, making sure that you can re-pitch the song when going to the second verse. Third, approach your task with confidence. Look at your audience eye-to-eye, clearly announce the number of the song or the selection so that everyone can hear. Hum the first note, take a deep breath, and then start singing. You have the opportunity and responsibility of leading women to worship in song. Be confident remembering the words of David, "Oh, sing to the Lord a new song! For He has done marvelous things" (Psalm 98:1).

Throughout my childhood and early teen years, brother Ralph Casey traveled throughout at least the eastern part of the United States conducting singing seminars or schools. In several of the congregations that I attended, I was privileged to attend these schools. Whether male or female, young or old, brother Casey set out to help the whole congregation understand the basic elements of music, including the time signatures, the musical notes or scales, and the sentiment of a song. The bulk of the information that I hope to share with you comes from these sessions that

I have attended as well as from the many years of experience that I have had in leading women in song at ladies days, in ladies Bible classes, and in retreats.

Music Basics

Before a person considers being a song leader, she must first become familiar with some of the basic elements of music. The two different sets of notes are arranged in the treble staff for the female voices and the bass staff for the male voices. The treble staff is where you will find the key the song is written in as well as the time signature of the song.

The song leader will use the key signature or the beginning note of the song to determine how high or low the song begins. A true student of music will know each key signature by the absence of or total of sharps and flats. However, the easiest way to determine where to blow the pitch is to look at the first soprano or highest note. In order to blow that pitch on a pitch pipe you must know what the lines and spaces stand for in a staff of music. The lines are e, g, b, d and f. The spaces are f, a, c, e. Once you locate the first note and look to see if it has a sharp or flat, you can then blow the pitch to begin the song.

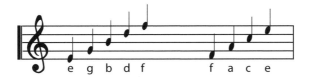

You must also be familiar with the various notes and rests to know whether it is a whole, half, quarter or eighth. Knowing the note or rest tells you how long to hold that note or how quickly to move to the next note. Some hymn books use what are called shaped notes; others use all round notes. A whole note has no filling and no stem or flag. A half note is not filled with a stem. The quarter note is filled with a stem. The eighth note adds one flag, and the sixteenth note adds two flags. Rests also have a specific shape to denote their time, but often the length of time a rest is held depends on the discretion of the song leader.

| whole note | half note | quarter note | eighth note | sixteenth note |

| whole rest | half rest | quarter rest | eighth rest | sixteenth rest |

In order for a song leader to be effective, the audience will need to know the time signatures and hand signals in order to be able to follow the leader. It does no good for the leader to direct if the participants do not know what the signals mean and thus how to follow effectively. Listed in the treble clef or the top score of music in our hymnals will be a number such as 2/4 or 3/4 or 6/8 or even 4/4. These numbers are called the time signatures.

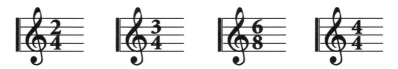

Beat Patterns

With each time signature, there is a universal beat pattern. There are actually four beat patterns that are commonly followed in congregational singing. They are double, triple, quadruple and sextuple.

In the simple double time signature the hand motion or beat pattern is simply down and up. Occasionally, some leaders will put a slight hook or bounce at the bottom of the down beat, but this hand motion will work with 2/2 or 2/4 or even 6/8. However, when you use the simple down and up beat with 6/8, it is called a compound double because there would be a count of 1, 2, 3 for the down and 4, 5, 6 going back up. This hand signal is the easiest to use and is usually the best to practice when someone is just beginning to learn to lead the singing. A familiar song with the 6/8 pattern is "Yield Not to Temptation." It starts on the downbeat.

The second beat pattern is called a triple and the beat pattern is down, out and up in the shape or motion of making a triangle in the air. This beat pattern is used for a time signature of 3/2, 3/4 or 3/8. It is also used with a 9/8 time signature, but it would be considered a compound triple rather than a simple. Once your hand comes to the bottom your outward motion can go in either direction depending on whether you are leading with your right hand or your left. Use what is most comfortable for you. The upward motion or last beat of the measure completes the formation of the triangle "in the air." A song with the 3/4 time signature is "O Master, Let Me Walk With Thee."

The third beat pattern is called the quadruple and is used with the 4/4 or 12/8 time signature. The beat pattern is down, in, out and up. As you beat the pattern the image that you are making in the air looks somewhat like a sail boat with the "in" motion being the hull of the boat. This pattern is the most difficult and should be worked on last after a person is comfortable directing the singing and the arm motions become more relaxed and natural. There seem to be more songs with the 4/4 time signature than the others. Some examples would be " 'Tis So Sweet to Trust in Jesus," "Give Me the Bible," "Take the Name of Jesus With You" and "When We All Get to Heaven."

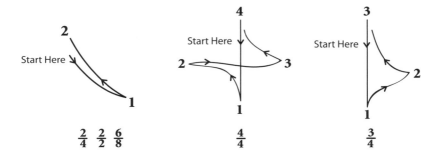

The most complex or difficult and rarely used beat pattern is called the sextuplet. This beat pattern is used with a 6/4 time signature. The pattern is down, in, in, out, up and up. This image when visualized is basically a larger sailboat with curves or waves in the bottom of the "hull" and the "sail." Vary rarely is this pattern used today with the 6/4 but rather the simple double of down and up is substituted.

Once we know the correct motion of the beat patterns, a person needs to know how to use the pattern and when the down beat occurs. The first motion downward in any beat pattern comes with the first note after the measure bar. The staff that the music is written on is also called a measure of music. The vertical lines are the measure bars. Within each measure there are to be either 2,3,4,6, etc. beats depending on what the time signature calls for. If the song begins with a few notes before the measure bar that is a partial count then the leaders first motion would not be the down beat. Most often the first motion would be an upward sweep to get ready for the down beat on the first note after the measure bar.

Tempo

As important as beat patterns are, they do not determine the tempo or speed of the song. Each song has a message that uplifts or encourages, teaches a lesson, or simply expresses our praises and adoration to our God. Depending on the sentiment of the song, it should be sung quickly or slowly or moderately. Some songs will actually have written above them specific terms to help the song leader know how the composer wanted that hymn to be sung. We can sing a song too fast or so slowly that we ruin the entire song and the message that it has to share.

Using Your Singing Ability to Serve

Well-known song leader Paul Brown, of Nashville, Tenn., says there are several ways in which women can make an important contribution to the music program of a local church or home.

• *Children's Bible Classes.* Singing should be a significant part in the teaching of children in Bible classes, which are usually taught by women. If there are teachers who are not singers, a woman may be assigned to sing with several classes as their music director, thus supporting the work of the teachers.

• *At Home.* Mothers singing to their own children are building the foundation for spiritual training in the home.

• *Funerals.* Often, there is a need for sopranos and altos to sing in a small group for funerals. This ministry provides comfort and encouragement through song to people who are going through a difficult time.

• *Women's Events.* Retreats, dorm devotionals and other special ladies events provide opportunities for women to lead other women in song. Because singing is called the universal language, women are needed to teach songs to both women and children in the mission field. Brown states:

> The words in the hymnbook are a vital teaching tool. A devotional time can be built by reading instead of singing the words to songs. The message of the hymn can be enriched by reading appropriate scriptures before singing. And studying the background of a hymn and its writer can add a new dimension of understanding a hymn's meaning.[1]

Songs for Women

When selecting hymns for a group of women to sing, try to avoid hymns that require bass or tenor leads, especially in the chorus, such as "Jesus Hold My Hand." If the words to the song have a specific meaning for the occasion, then omit the chorus to avoid the need for men's voices. Most women would rather sing a hymn that is meditative, using a close blending of the soprano and alto. Some suggestions for women's voices are:

"As the Deer Panteth for the Water"	"Amazing Grace"
"How Beautiful Heaven Must Be"	"At Calvary"
"A Hill Called Mount Calvary"	"A Wonderful Savior"
"Above the Bright Blue"	"Fairest Lord Jesus"
"His Eye Is on the Sparrow"	"Be Still and Know"

"All the Way My Savior Leads Me"   "An Empty Mansion"
"Are You Coming to Jesus Tonight?"   "Be With Me Lord"
"I Gave My Life for Thee"   "Beyond the Sunset"
"Beneath the Cross of Jesus"   "Blest Be the Tie"
"Day Is Dying in the West"   "Buried With Christ"
"Did You Think to Pray?"   "Does Jesus Care?"
"Dear Lord and Father of Mankind"   "Crossing the Bar"
"Do You Know My Jesus?"   "Face to Face"
"God Will Take Care of You"   "Father of Mercies"
"Have Thine Own Way, Lord"   "Flee As a Bird"
"Hark! The Gentle Voice of Jesus"   "Give Me the Bible"
"Heaven Holds All to Me"   "How Great Thou Art"
"How Sweet, How Heavenly"   "I Believe in Jesus"
"I Have Found a Friend in Jesus"   "Ivory Palaces"
"I Love to Tell the Story"   "I Love the Lord"
"I Need Thee Every Hour"   "I'd Rather Have Jesus"
"Is Thy Heart Right With God?"   "More About Jesus"
"Jesus Is All the World to Me"   "Lead Me to Calvary"
"Lead Me to Some Soul Today"   "In the Morning of Joy"
"Let Every Heart Rejoice and Sing"   "How Long Has It Been?"
"Let Him Have His Way With Thee"   "Just As I Am"
"Let Jesus Come Into Your Heart"   "Blessed Assurance"
"Let the Beauty of Jesus Be Seen"   "Into My Heart"

Conclusion

In summary, I would like to share some wonderful comments Dan R. Owen made about our singing:

> By capturing the mood of a particular song and enunciating the words of that song in such a way as to convey clearly the message, we can use words written by other people to convey our own sentiments and emotions to our God and to others. Singing songs with passion can bring new life even to old songs. The attitude of the "worship" (song) leader is very important to the attitude of all who are present. Preachers and scripture readers and song leaders and prayer leaders are

trying to take the people somewhere in their thoughts and emotions. They will go where we take them, so let us sing with the kind of emphasis and emotion that will take them where God wants them to go in praise and worship.[2]

Activities

1. Purchase or check your church library for books of stories about the hymns in our songbooks. Some examples are: *A Song Is Born* by Robert Taylor, *101 Hymn Stories* by Kenneth W. Osbeck, or *Then Sings My Soul* by Robert Morgan. Select one of the stories of a favorite hymn and share it with your class. Talk about the words to the song and how knowing about the author and why the song was written enhances our devotion. You might also want to try searching the internet or visiting a website like www.cyberhymnal.com.

2. Purchase a songbook for yourself or borrow some for your ladies class or retreat. Go through the songbook and see how many songs are taken directly from Scripture. Some selections might be: "Great Is Thy Faithfulness" from Lamentations 3:23-24; "The Lord Is My Shepherd" from Psalm 23; and "O Heart Bowed Down With Sorrow" from Matthew 11:28-30. Read the verses from the Bible, and then read the song aloud.

3. Using a songbook, turn to any song and look at the treble staff. Identify the different types of notes pictured on page 114. How many beats does the whole note receive when the song is in 4/4 time? Why is the tempo of the song important to worship?

4. In order to get women to sing along, you might try leading them first in songs for children. Most of these songs have simple melodies and are easily sung. Try "Jesus Loves Me," "Into My Heart," and "Rejoice in the Lord Always" to warm up your audience before moving to another selection.

Chapter 11

Growing
Pains

Janie Craun

We seldom went to the doctor when I was growing up. A bone that might be fractured was wrapped in a home-made splint, and cuts to our bare feet were soaked in kerosene. My mama doctored us with cough syrup made from honey and vinegar. Once the doctor made a house call bringing "real" medicine; otherwise I can remember only a handful of visits made to his office.

As a rule, whenever we had aches that were not accompanied by prolonged fever, my mother would tell us kids that those were just "growing pains." Why we had to have growing pains puzzled me, but our parents insisted that everyone had them, and I accepted the fact that a little pain was the price one paid to become a grown-up.

Growing Up Spiritually

The same is true when it comes to growing up spiritually. It isn't easy to become a full-grown, mature Christian. "No pain, no gain," seems to be the rule.

Mama consoled me by saying that my growing pains were nature's way of making me bigger. My bones were getting larger and stronger, and my muscles were stretching to catch up. Growing up in Christ means that we have to s-t-r-e-t-c-h from time to time. Getting out of our comfort zone involves discomfort, but it is necessary if we are to achieve new heights. The woman who never grows will be a stunted Christian and will not glorify her Lord.

Do you remember when you were born? Spiritually, that is. It all began when you were conceived. The seed of God's Word was planted in your receptive heart, and it resulted in your being born into the family of God. Peter wrote about this process saying, "[L]ove one another fervently with a pure heart, having been born again, not of corruptible seed but incorruptible, through the word of God which lives and abides forever" (1 Peter 1:22-23).

That verse tells us that we were made to live eternally because the germ of life within us is incorruptible. Unless we choose to terminate our own spiritual life, we really will live forever as God's child.

People sometimes ask, "Are you a born-again Christian?" That term is redundant. No one can become a Christian without being born again. Jesus explained this to Nicodemus saying, "Most assuredly, I say to you, unless one is born again, he cannot see the kingdom of God" (John 3:3). Furthermore, Jesus specified that "unless one is born of water and the Spirit, he cannot enter the kingdom of God" (v. 5).

Our new life as a child of God originated with His Holy Spirit (John 6:63) and was ushered into the world by means of water. Titus states that our salvation involves both, saying "not by works of righteousness which we have done, but according to His mercy He saved us, through the washing of regeneration [rebirth] and renewing of the Holy Spirit" (Titus 3:5).

As newborn babies, once we got our first taste of milk we couldn't get enough of it. When I was a young mother, I loved nursing my own babies. It was so satisfying to see them filled and content. So, too, the new Christian, having been born of the Spirit, longs to feed upon the Word of God. If she has no interest in feeding, she will become weak. Death can even result from a condition called "failure to thrive."

Peter encourages Christians saying, "as newborn babes, desire the pure milk of the word, that you may grow thereby, if indeed you have tasted that the Lord is gracious" (1 Peter 2:2-3). He sums up his second epistle with a final reminder that one must continue to "grow in the grace and knowledge of our Lord and Savior Jesus Christ" (2 Peter 3:18).

In the first century, God supplied the infant church with spiritual gifts to assist them in their development. The gifts lasted until the church grew up, that is, until congregations had acquired the maturity that results from familiarity with God's Word. By the time the apostles and other inspired writers had all died and those to whom they had imparted spiritual gifts had also died, the church had acquired all of the New Testament Scriptures and was mature enough to resist false teaching using the written Word.

Paul foresaw that time, saying that the gifts were designed to equip the saints until the church should "come to the unity of the faith and of the knowledge of the Son of God, to a perfect [mature] man, to the measure of the stature of the fullness of Christ" (Ephesians 4:13). He continued, advising them to "no longer be children, tossed to and fro and carried about with every wind of doctrine ... but, speaking the truth in love ... grow up in all things into Him who is the head – Christ" (vv. 14-15).

Although none of us expects to reach the level of perfection that characterized our Lord, it is a worthy goal. Jesus continued to grow spiritually from an early age. As a result, He became "strong in spirit, filled with wisdom; and the grace of God was upon Him" (Luke 2:40). Like Him, we must advance beyond a level of spiritual adolescence to grow in God's favor.

What Is Required?

There was a time when people thought it improper for a woman to be too educated, but the Bible's admonitions to grow were not written to men only. Christian women need to become students of the Word. Mary was criticized by her sister Martha for sitting at the feet of Jesus and neglecting the domestic duties expected of her (Luke 10:38-42), but Jesus praised Mary and said she had chosen a good thing.

Even today a woman may be criticized for being "too studious." It's never wrong, however, for a woman to sit at the Lord's feet. Knowing the Scriptures well will open up many opportunities to share the gospel – and without violating the limitations that God has placed upon us.

One good example is Priscilla, who along with her husband taught an eloquent and dynamic evangelist the way of God more accurately (Acts 18:26). They did it privately, by taking him aside. In the Greek text her name is mentioned first, indicating that perhaps she had a significant part in the teaching. It suggests that Priscilla was a good student of the Word.

Being well-versed in the Bible opens doors for ministering to others in many ways, including these:

• *Teaching children.* In ancient times women did most of the nurturing of their children in their formative years. After the child was weaned, at perhaps 4 or 5 years of age, fathers assumed the responsibility of training their sons, and mothers continued to teach their daughters as long as they remained under their roof. Women, as well as men, were told to teach their grandchildren (Deuteronomy 4:9; 6:2; 2 Timothy 1:5).

Today single women also have a tremendous opportunity to influence children because they may have advantages married women do not. They may have the time and resources that enable them to further their studies and to participate in teacher-training workshops, mission campaigns, and activities such as Bible bowls, Lads to Leaders/Leaderettes, etc. When teaching children, however, remember that the primary objective is to instruct rather than to entertain. Take your lessons from the Scriptures so that your classes will consist of solid nourishment rather than junk food.

• *Teaching young women.* There are some things that only an older woman with experience can teach a younger woman.

Among these are how to be a loving wife and mother and a good homemaker. Too many young wives and mothers rely upon television or the tabloids for advice. One popular "expert" in child-rearing advises that parents should not use authority in dealing with their children because children resent it and want to limit their behavior themselves.[1] As ridiculous as it sounds, many parents believe that if an expert says it is so, it must be so. An effective teacher draws from the wisdom of Scripture while being knowledgeable about current trends and attitudes.

Titus also mentioned practical details that young women need to hear from older women, such as the need for discretion and chastity (Titus 2:3-5). Teens and young women need straight talk about what is appropriate in the areas of dress, conversation and sexuality. They are most likely to listen to someone who is a good role model, who knows how to dress attractively but modestly, who is articulate and knowledgeable about the Scriptures, and who demonstrates the fruit of the Spirit in her own life. These are qualities to be cultivated in those who would teach this age group. You may need to acquaint yourself with the music, styles and entertainment that so strongly influence other young women but teach them from the Scripture to "have an answer for those who take pride in appearance and not in heart" (2 Corinthians 5:12 NASB).

• *Teaching women who are your peers.* It is often difficult to find women willing to teach their peers. Maturity involves preparing ourselves to become teachers at some point rather than students only (Hebrews 5:12-14). There is a sore need for more of us to do so. We need more women who will equip themselves in these and other areas, such as:

(1) Leading women in prayer and in song. Prayers uttered from a woman's heart are often deep and intuitive. We women need to hear each other pray and be encouraged by the beauty of other female voices raised in praise to God.

(2) Teaching a ladies Bible class. Most women are more comfortable and will participate more readily in a class taught by another woman.

(3) Speaking at ladies days and lectureships. Women enjoy the opportunity to fellowship with others and to be edified by sisters who understand their needs.

(4) Writing study books and devotional materials. Whether doing a topical or a textual study, many women prefer material written from a woman's viewpoint. Publishers of brotherhood books and magazines are always looking for Christian women who can write.

(5) Teaching through Bible correspondence. Again, a working knowledge of the Bible allows a woman to teach others from around the world without leaving her home. There are opportunities to teach foreigners through ESL classes (English as a Second Language) using the Bible as a textbook.

(6) Creating websites operated by women for women in the church. For those with computer skills these sites offer the chance to share information and teaching with other women.

With so many avenues open to us, we may wonder why more women do not avail themselves of the opportunity to develop their leadership talents. Maybe you have had one or more of these concerns at times.

"Is It Scriptural?"

Over the last half-century the modern feminist movement has made an impact upon society in a number of ways. Some of them have been good, such as the struggle that gave women the right to vote or the efforts to bring about equal pay for equal work. In the early 1960s, "male bashing" became a popular pastime of the radical feminists, some of whom even called for the end of marriage as an institution.

Other, more moderate feminists, simply wanted equality in all areas including the running of the home and the church. Those who called themselves "Christian" feminists fought for, and in many cases succeeded in winning, leadership roles in their respective churches which included the right to lead in worship and to hold positions of oversight. This movement has filtered into the Lord's church, causing some to question New Testament passages that clearly define a woman's role as one of subjection in these areas. In several congregations today, women now serve as preachers, elders and worship leaders.

Those who hold the Bible to be the inspired Word of God have resisted this trend, believing it to be contrary to God's expressed will. We realize that women in the early church were actively involved in the spreading of truth. They prophesied (Acts 21:9; 1 Corinthians 11:5); they taught other women (Titus 2:3-5); they worked on behalf of the church in unspecified ways (vv. 6, 12); and they supported the spread of the gospel financially (Luke 8:1-3; Romans 16:1-2).

Everett Ferguson, in summarizing these areas, has written that "Christians must confess that churches have not always utilized women as fully as these passages indicate they were involved in apostolic days." But he concludes that when it comes to abandoning scriptural standards concerning male and female roles, "both reactions are wrong. Cultural practices and societal preferences should not lead the church into either error, either placing undue restrictions on women's work or not respecting Biblical limitations." [2]

In our desire to respect biblical limitations, however, it is possible that many sisters have feared to channel their talents into ministries that are tailored to women. As a result, their talents remain hidden and good works go undone.

"I'm Not Qualified"

Teresa Hampton, in her book *Leading Ladies*, suggests that women may labor under several misconceptions when it comes to leading other women. Among them are these:

(1) A good leader must be an extrovert or have an outgoing personality;

(2) A good leader must have an active, supportive spouse;

(3) Leadership positions are best suited for those of a particular age; and

(4) External attributes like beauty and grace make or break a good leader. [3]

I would add that some also feel that a good leader must have a formal education or that she must be more talented than the average woman. Too often, we compare ourselves to others and feel that we fall short of someone else's abilities. As a result we never develop our own talents.

"I'm Afraid."

No sooner had Adam and Eve sinned by disobeying God until the devil succeeded in filling them with fear (Genesis 3:10). Since that time, Satan has used fear effectively for manipulation.

Many biblical heroes experienced fear at one time or another. Abraham may have had doubts about his calling (Genesis 15:1). Isaac needed reassurance that God was with him (Genesis 26:24). Jacob feared his own brother (Genesis 32:11). Moses dreaded the commission God had given him, offering every excuse he could think of before begging, "Lord, please send someone else" (Exodus 4:13 ESV). God had to encourage Joshua three times to be strong and courageous as Israel's new leader (Joshua 1:6, 7, 9, 18). Paul found his ministry so difficult at times that he literally trembled in weakness and in fear (1 Corinthians 2:3).

So you and I aren't the only ones who have sometimes felt intimidated, even terrified, at the prospect of taking on a new responsibility. We can only imagine the anxiety that must have gripped Queen Esther as she prepared to risk her own life for her people (Esther 4:16). Fear and anxiety are "pains" that may take a lifetime to outgrow. Think, however, how the course of history would be changed if the great men and women of the Bible had given in to their fears. Jesus told a parable about a man who chose to play it safe and bury his opportunity because he was afraid (Matthew 25:24-25). Faith is the willingness to rely upon God rather than upon ourselves.

"I Haven't the Time."

A young Christian mother confided to me that she is concerned about the fact that her children are not very involved in Bible classes and other programs of the church. She worries that her work schedule and their extra-curricular activities have kept them from participating more, and she adds that she, herself, does not know the Bible as she ought to. She doesn't think her husband will ever become a deacon because they are just too busy.

This young mother is sincere, but her priorities are misplaced. She wants to grow spiritually but can't seem to find the time to devote to it. With a job, keeping up the house, involving the kids in sports and other activities, entertainment and her own personal interests, she feels guilty because she has little time for in-depth Bible study or participation in ministry – let alone for developing her leadership skills. Does this describe anyone you know?

Despite Jesus' admonition to "seek first the kingdom of God and His righteousness" (Matthew 6:33), we struggle to keep first things first. Too many children grow up and leave the church because it was never the focal point of their lives. Too late, many of us may wish we had taken the time to become the person God intended us to be.

"I'm Not Interested."

Seldom do we hear this reason stated with such candor. More often, apathy reveals itself in intermittent church attendance and in half-hearted participation in worship. The apathetic Christian has lost any real desire to grow, and her involvement in the church has become routine. Although she may not admit it, she finds the worship boring; and only guilt prompts her to keep going through the motions. Sad to say, many in the pews appear to be in this group. They have lost their spiritual appetite, and if it does not return, they will soon fall away altogether. This is how apathy works. In the parable of the talents, the one who buried his gift suffered more than a missed opportunity. He lost the little that he started with.

What Now?

Having decided, then, that developing your leadership potential is not unscriptural, that you are qualified to lead in some area, that growth should be a priority in your life, and that fear can be overcome – how do you get started? Hopefully, after reading the previous chapters, you have a good understanding of the many avenues open to you, and you want to explore the possibilities. One thing remains. You must set a goal and go to work to attain it. More growing pains! But remember, your spiritual body is stretching itself, working to make you a bigger person in God's sight.

As you begin, keep these things in mind:

• Be realistic. Don't expect success overnight.
• Choose an area in which you have a strong desire to succeed.
• Set one goal at a time.
• Let someone know about your desire.
• Share your fears with someone you view as a role model.
• Ask for advice from those who seem competent.
• Ask others to pray for/with you.
• Find a partner who also needs encouragement.
• Practice reading/speaking/praying aloud at home.
• Don't expect perfection. Allow for some blunders.
• Learn to laugh at yourself.
• Be persistent. Don't give up.
• Give God the glory for the successes you enjoy.

If you think this seems overwhelming, remember Rome wasn't built in a day. Tack this verse in a prominent place: "I can do all things through Christ who strengthens me" (Philippians 4:13). Remember that Paul wrote these words during a time of imprisonment, when many obstacles stood in his way. This godly man, who sometimes trembled at the things God directed him to do, also lived by the rule: "I press toward the goal" (3:14).

Activities

Choose one of the ministries discussed in earlier chapters that you have not attempted before. Using this worksheet, check each activity as you complete it.

Name_____

1. My goal is to _____

2. I want to do this because _____
    _____

3. I have shared my desire with _____
    _____

4. My role model is _____
    _____

5. I have confided to her that _____
    _____

6. My fear is that _____
    _____

7. I have received the following advice: _____
    _____
    _____

8. I have asked _____
    to pray for/with me.

9. My partner, _____,
    has a goal of _____

10. I have practiced _____
    at home.

11. A specific area in which I want to improve my delivery
    is _____

12. I can laugh at myself when I blunder. Yes _____ No _____

13. I did it! I led in reading/praying/singing/speaking/
    other for the first time.

    _____   _____
    (signed)   (dated)

14. Write a short prayer, thanking God for the opportunity to exercise your talent.

_____

_____

_____

_____

_____

Helpful Resources

Grammar/Style Books

The Little, Brown Handbook (Harpercollins College Division; 5th edition; January 1997) Provides comprehensive coverage of writing, research and grammar, with detailed discussions of critical thinking and argument, using computers and the Internet for writing and research, and the latest guidelines for citing sources correctly in MLA, APA, CMS, CSE and COS styles.

Chicago Manual of Style (University of Chicago Press; 15th edition; August 1, 2003) For writers, editors, publishers, proofreaders, indexers, copyrighters and designers. Covers publishing formats, editorial style and method, book design and production, and everything in between.

In addition to books, the Manual now also treats journals and electronic publications. All chapters are written for the electronic age, with advice on how to prepare and edit manuscripts online, handle copyright and permissions issues raised by technology, and cite electronic and online sources.

Quotations

www.bartleby.com

www.gutenberg.com

Bartlett's Familiar Quotations by John Bartlett, (Little, Brown and Company; 17th edition; November 2002)

Biblical Translations and Resources

New Strong's Exhaustive Concordance by James Strong and John R. Kohlenberger III (Hendrickson).

Vine's Complete Expository Dictionary of Old and New Testament Words by W.E. Vine (Thomas Nelson, 1996)

www.biblegateway.com

Restoration Serials Index – www.acu.edu/rsi/index.php.

Gospel Advocate Bible Study Software, Deluxe Edition (Gospel Advocate Co., 2005) – Includes 9 Bible translations, *Gospel Advocate New Testament Commentaries, Johnson's Notes*, many other commentaries and resources.

Urban Legends

www.urbanlegends.about.com

www.snopes.com/info/search

www.truthorfiction.com

Hymn Words and Origins

www.cyberhymnal.com

Dictionary – Merriam Webster

www.m-w.com

Copyright Information

www.copyright.gov

www.wiley.com/legacy/authors/guidelines/stmguides/3frames. htm – This site is specifically prepared for Wiley staff members, but has a clear set of guidelines for using copyrighted material.

Endnotes

Chapter 1

1. It is not the purpose of this book to discuss the role of women, but I would encourage you to study that topic. *What About the Women?* by Cynthia Dianne Guy (Nashville, TN: Gospel Advocate, 2005) is an excellent book for that purpose.

2. Frederic Martini and Edwin Bartholomew, *Essentials of Anatomy & Physiology*, 4th Ed. (New York: Benjamin Cummings, 2007).

3. Pamela Stewart, *Evangelistic Women, A Study of Women's Ministries* (Kearney, NE: Morris, 2000).

Chapter 4

1. Gary Smalley and John Trent, Ph.D., *The Gift of Honor* (New York: Inspirational Press, 1987) 280.

2. Karen Pruitt, "Modern-Day Macedonians," *Christian Woman* Sept./Oct. 2006: 15.

3. Joanna Weaver, *Having a Mary Heart in a Martha World* (Colorado Springs, CO: Waterbrook, 2000) 10.

4. Weaver 10.

5. Virelle Kidder, "The Love Squad," *Stories for a Kindred Heart*, eds. Alice Gray and Barbara Baumgardner (Sisters, OR: Multnomah, 2000) 58.

6. Kidder 59.

7. Frederick Drimmer, ed., *A Friend Is Someone Special* (Norwalk, CT: C.R. Gibson, 1975) 4.

8. Emilie Barnes, *The Spirit of Loveliness* (Eugene, OR: Harvest House, 1992) 126.

9. Bernie Arnold, "Picnic in the Parlor," *Christian Woman* May/June 2003: 13-15.

Chapter 6

1. Mark Galli and Craig Brian Larson, *Preaching That Connects* (Grand Rapids, MI: Zondervan, 1994) 26.

2. James Braga, *How to Prepare Bible Messages* (Sisters, OR: Multnomah, 1981) 94.

3. H.C. Brown Jr., H. Gordon Clinard, Jesse J. Northcutt and Al Fasol, *Steps to the Sermon* (Nashville, TN: Broadman & Holman, 1996) 134, 135.

4. J.J. Turner, *Standing Before an Audience* (West Monroe, LA: Central, 1982) 21.

5. Braga 229.

6. Turner 27.

Chapter 7

1. Thomas H. Holland, *Sermon Design and Delivery*, 2nd ed. (Brentwood, TN: Penman, 1967) 65.

2. Charlton Hillis, "Women's Bible Class: Fluff or Substance?", *Gospel Advocate* March 2002: 21.

3. R. Stafford North, *Preaching: Man and Method* (Oklahoma City: OCC, 1971) 86.

4. Herbert Lockyer, *The Women of the Bible* (Grand Rapids, MI: Zondervan, 1967) 155.

5. Lockyer 157.

6. Nick Hamilton, "Sarah Waited on God – Hebrews 11:11," *Freed-Hardeman University Lectures*, ed. David Lipe, vol. 69 (Henderson, TN: FHU, 2001) 160.

7. L. Katherine Cook, "Laughter of Hope, Laughter of Joy: A Mother's Day Sermon," *Christian Ministry* May 1986: 31.

8. Charles W. Carter, *Hebrews, The Wesleyan Bible Commentary*, vol. 6. (Grand Rapids: Eerdmans, 1966) 147.

9. Donald G. Miller, *The Way to Biblical Preaching* (Nashville, TN: Abingdon, 1957) 53

10. Donald Guthrie, *The Letter to the Hebrews: An Introduction and Commentary* (Grand Rapids, MI: Eerdmans, 1983) 232.

11. Charles L. Brown, "Sarah, An Example for Modern Women," *East Tennessee School of Preaching Lectures*, ed. James Meadows, vol. 27 (Knoxville, TN: ETSP, 2001) 476.

12. Louis Rushmore, "Homiletics: Sermon Preparation," *Christian Bible Teacher* June 2001: 130.

13. North 71.

14. Braga 21-22.

15. Braga 124.

16. John H. Walton, *Genesis, The NIV Application Commentary*, gen. ed. Terry Muck (Grand Rapids, MI: Zondervan, 2001) 446.

17. Albert Barnes, *Barnes' Notes on the New Testament* (Grand Rapids, MI: Kregel, 1962) 1321.

18. North 70.

19. Rushmore 130.

20. Andrew W. Blackwood, *The Preparation of Sermons* (Nashville, TN: Abingdon, 1948) 115.

21. Braga 103.

22. Velma Hardin, "All Kneecaps Look Alike," letter, *Christian Woman* May/June 2000: 49.

23. North 100.

24. Lottie Beth Hobbs, *Daughters of Eve* (Ft. Worth: Harvest, 1963) 19.

25. Walton 446.

26. Eugenia Price, *God Speaks to Women Today* (Grand Rapids, MI: Zondervan, 1964) 25.

27. Lockyer 158.

28. Cook 31.

29. Bobbie Cramer Jobe, *Sarah's Story* (Abilene, TX: Quality, 1986) 38.

30. Bruce K. Waltke, *Genesis: A Commentary* (Grand Rapids, MI: Zondervan, 2001) 268.

31. Gordon J. Wenham, *Genesis 16-50, Word Biblical Commentary*, vol. 2., gen. eds. David A. Hubbard and Glenn W. Barker (Dallas: Word, 1994) 48.

32. Richard A. Spencer, "Hebrews 11:1-3, 8-16," *Interpretation* July 1995: 242.

33. North 102.

34. North 103.

35. North 105.

36. Blackwood 107.

37. Neale Pryor, "Abraham: Believing the Promises," *Harding University Lectures*, vol. 68 (Searcy, AR: HU, 1991) 53.

38. Jobe 38.

39. Brown 476.

40. Rushmore 131.

41. Eva Shaw, *The Craft of Magazine Writing*, Ed2go online course, lesson 3 <http://www.ed2go.com/index.html>.

Chapter 9

1. Michael Burlingame, ed., *Lincoln Observed: The Civil War Dispatches of Noah Brooks* (Baltimore: Johns Hopkins, 1998) 210.

2. J.C. Lambert, *International Standard Bible Encyclopedia*, ed. James Orr (Peabody, MA: Hendrickson, 2002) 2430.

3. Ancil Jenkins, *Lord, Teach Us to Pray* (Nashville, TN: Gospel Advocate, 1988) 9.

4. C.F. Cruse, *Eusebius' Ecclesiastical History: Complete and Unabridged*, Book 5 (Peabody, MA: Hendrickson, 1998) 76.

5. Guy N. Woods, *James*, *New Testament Commentaries*, vol. 12 (1985; Nashville, TN: Gospel Advocate, 1991) 41.

6. Guy N. Woods, *I and II Peter, I, II and III John, and Jude*, *New Testament Commentaries*, vol. 13 (1954; Nashville, TN: Gospel Advocate, 1991) 63.

Chapter 10

1. Paul Brown, personal interview, 21 Sept. 2006.

2. Dan R. Owen, "The Manner of Our Singing," *Gospel Advocate* April 2006: 32.

Chapter 12

1. Thomas Gordon, *Parenting Effectiveness Training: The Proven Program for Raising Responsible Children* (New York: Three Rivers, 2000). Quoted by James Dobson, *The New Strong-Willed Child* (Wheaton, IL: Tyndale House, 2004) 54.

2. Everett Ferguson, *Women in the Church* (Chickasha, OK: Yeomen, 2003), 10.

3. Teresa Hampton, *Leading Ladies: Willing Hearts, Willing Hands* (Huntsville, AL: Publishing Designs, 2001) 12-15.

About the Authors

Joyce Bloomingburg is an assistant professor at Freed-Hardeman University in the department of behavioral and family studies as well as the director of the nursery school program at FHU. Joyce teaches cradle roll class at the Henderson, Tenn., Church of Christ, participates in Lads-to-Leaders, and teaches at Horizons at FHU as needed. She and her husband, Randy, have two daughters.

Amanda Box is the communication and program coordinator for Mississippi Forestry Association in Jackson, Miss. For the last 14 years she has taught communication and speech classes at Freed-Hardeman University and conducts online courses for two community colleges in Mississippi. She serves as a national consultant for business and industry, using an interactive presentation style to teach specific communication skills to diverse groups. Amanda's husband, Chuck, is a baseball coach. They have two children.

Debbie Bumbalough is the vice president of sales at Gospel Advocate Co., editor of *Ideashop* magazine, on the staff of *Christian Woman* magazine, and a consultant for Heritage of Faith curriculum. Debbie attended Lipscomb University and has taken classes at the Nashville School of Biblical Studies. She conducts teacher training seminars and is a frequent speaker at ladies days and lectureships. She has worked in mission campaigns for the last 11 years. Debbie and her husband, Mike, have three grown children and seven grandchildren.

Sue Crabtree has master's degrees from Auburn University and Regions University. She has taught education classes and Bible classes at Faulkner University in Montgomery, Ala., for 25 years. Sue has written two books: *Let's Be Great Teachers* and *4000 Years in Thirteen Weeks*. Her husband, James, is a retired Christian educator. Jim and Sue work in the Inner City Ministry in Montgomery.

Janie Craun, editor of *Christian Woman* magazine, has been involved with publishing for many years. She has written articles for *Christian Bible Teacher*, Sunday school lessons for Lambert Book House, and is the author of a book, *Heirlooms: Bible Keepsakes New and Old*. Janie often speaks for ladies days and retreats. Janie has a bachelor's degree from Lipscomb University and is a graduate of the Nashville School of Preaching and Biblical Studies. She was an elementary school teacher for 18 years and has served as preschool director at Walnut Street Church of Christ. She has also taught ladies classes at the White Bluff Church of Christ for 15 years. Janie's husband, Karl, is an elder of the White Bluff Church of Christ. They have two grown children and one grandchild.

Cynthia Dianne Guy is a wife, mother, free-lance writer, and adjunct instructor at Heritage Christian University in Florence, Ala. Cynthia has bachelor's and master's degrees in Bible from HCU and is pursuing a doctorate in Christian women's studies. She is the author of *What About the Women?*, published by Gospel

Advocate. Her husband, Steven, is minister of the Booneville, Miss., Church of Christ and professor of homiletics at HCU. They have four grown sons.

Melissa Lester, a graduate of Lipscomb University, is the author of the book *Giving for All It's Worth* and a frequent speaker at ladies events. She has served as a contributing editor to *Christian Woman* and *Ideals* magazines. Her husband, Joe, is a professor at Faulkner University's Jones School of Law in Montgomery, Ala. Melissa and Joe are the parents of four children. They are members of the University Church of Christ, where Joe is a deacon and Melissa is a Bible class teacher.

Rosemary McKnight, an elementary school teacher, has taught a ladies Bible class for 20 years. A speaker for ladies days, she is also the author of two books, *Those Who Wait* and *I Love Me, I Love Me Not*. Her husband, Gary, is an elder and the director of choral activities at Freed-Hardeman University. The McKnights live in Henderson, Tenn., and have two grown sons.

Pamela Stewart, dean of women at the Bear Valley Bible Institute of Denver, also teaches "Women's Ministries and Evangelism" classes. She is a graduate of the women's program for preachers' wives at the White's Ferry Road School of Biblical Studies in West Monroe, La., and has earned a bachelor's degree in biblical studies from Bear Valley. Pamela is often a guest speaker for ladies days, workshops and retreats. She is the author of the book *Evangelistic Women,* writes for the *Rocky Mountain Christian,* and has written for many other magazines. Pamela is married to Bill Stewart, an instructor and director of development at Bear Valley. She and her husband have done mission work in many foreign countries. They have four grown children and 10 grandchildren.

Dwina Willis received her undergraduate degree in biology from Freed-Hardeman and Harding universities. She received an MSE in biology from the University of Central Arkansas and an MM from FHU. Dwina teaches freshman biology and women's Bible classes at Freed-Hardeman University. She is married to David Willis (USAF retired), who serves as an elder at the Henderson Church of Christ. They have three children and two grandchildren.